Burning Temple

Burning Temple

Facing Our Anger at God

Chad Marcus Freeman

WIPF & STOCK · Eugene, Oregon

BURNING TEMPLE
Facing Our Anger at God

Copyright © 2016 Chad Marcus Freeman. All rights reserved. Except for brief quotations in critical publications or reviews, no part of this book may be reproduced in any manner without prior written permission from the publisher. Write: Permissions, Wipf and Stock Publishers, 199 W. 8th Ave., Suite 3, Eugene, OR 97401.

Wipf & Stock
An Imprint of Wipf and Stock Publishers
199 W. 8th Ave., Suite 3
Eugene, OR 97401

www.wipfandstock.com

PAPERBACK ISBN: 978-1-5326-1107-0
HARDCOVER ISBN: 978-1-5326-1109-4
EBOOK ISBN: 978-1-5326-1108-7

Manufactured in the U.S.A.   DECEMBER 6, 2016

All Scripture quotations are taken from the Holy Bible, English Standard Version® (ESV®) Copyright © 2001 by Crossway, a publishing ministry of Good News Publishers. All rights reserved.
ESV® Permanent Text Edition® (2016)

To Leah, for more reasons than I know how to say.

Contents

Acknowledgments | ix
Introduction | xi

Part I: A Hemorrhaging Faith
    Chapter 1   More than We Know | 3
    Chapter 2   We Made a Home | 11
    Chapter 3   What Is Our Anger at God? | 19

Part II: The Story of Our Anger at God
    Chapter 4   Frozen Grief | 31
    Chapter 5   Too Tired to Think, Too Far to See | 41
    Chapter 6   Stories Told & Secondhand Truths | 49

Part III: The Story of an Abandoned God
    Chapter 7   Where Is Jesus? | 65
    Chapter 8   God's Breaking | 77
    Chapter 9   God's Resolution | 97

Part IV: Finding Our Story & Place
    Chapter 10   Between Reality & the Quest for Satisfaction | 117
    Chapter 11   Between Now & Then | 127
    Chapter 12   Between Us & Him | 132

Bibliography | 139

Acknowledgments

WHILE WRITING AS A "job" I am repeatedly brutalized by Steven Pressfield's truth that writing is work. Hard work. And I have needed help to complete this meager work you now hold. My wife, Leah, experienced the realities of the life this book only describes. I am grateful for the love, trust, and patience she gives to me as I chased down this dream. My daughter, Ruby, gives me the silly laughter and distractions I need when the work is overwhelming. I hope one day this book will help her better understand her inconsistent father.

I am grateful to John Mark Hallman for a friendship I consistently fail to deserve. His encouragement and authenticity give me courage. Ken Quinn answered a sacred calling, and I am forever changed by his faithfulness to his work. Dr. Adrian Smith showed me what it looks like to be authentically yourself as he taught me in seminary, befriended me over shepherd's pie, and made professional introductions on my behalf. I owe my masters degree and this, my first published book, to him. Ranz Nelson spent hours doing mountains of editing for this dyslexic author. His friendship and guidance make me a better writer.

At the end of a work such as this, I cannot help but be grateful for a God who goes far beyond "not giving up on me." He is a God who chooses to face personal sorrow and pain for the sake of those he loves. He loves me. After years of my anger and bitterness, and now from a place of peace and acceptance, it is difficult to take for granted the thankfulness that swells inside me for his continual embrace.

Introduction

THERE IS NOTHING ABSTRACT about being angry at God. It is not an interesting topic to explore. For me, it is a painful pilgrimage through places both near and far. It is a lonely trek through pain and bewilderment. We stumble over hidden emotions and sorrows, questioning what we believe about God and ourselves. It takes a long time to understand that our questions were not an enemy. It takes even longer to find the trust to believe that God is not our enemy either.

If you have picked up this book, you know something of what I am describing. A lonely journey that feels futile in the face of the questions closing in. Can God be trusted? Is he who professional Christians say he is (when they can agree about anything important)? Does he really love us? Where is he when things hit the fan? Is he worth our praise when he allows suffering and sorrow to steal and pummel those clinging to hope?

After years of hurting, I could no longer keep these questions to myself. After abandonment, abuse, a failed marriage, and lost job opportunities, I began screaming my questions. These questions made it nearly impossible to sit through seminary classes without both rage and tears gushing out of me. Adding insult to injury, these questions tainted every pastoral job interview I went through. It was not until I sat with a professional counselor that I began to really trust some of the things I had been preaching about God over the years. I started to grieve the pain I denied for much of my adult life. I stopped hiding more than I stood in the shadows. I was confronted with how beauty and suffering tend to grow together in this world. But ultimately, I was confounded by a simple truth: I cannot be angry at God without also being angry at Jesus.

This book is an attempt to map out the broad strokes of a journey we all must make. Your steps will look different from mine, but your feet will trudge through similar valleys and peaks. You might travel faster, but it won't be a quick trip. You might start in a different spot, but the journey ends at Jesus's cross. Not all of our questions will be answered, but not all of our questions are as important as we think. We have already experienced enough guilt and shame for one lifetime, so don't expect any more to be delivered in the pages that follow. We are told that we are living temples of God. And yet, we have set ourselves ablaze with our anger at him. But the flames do not have to continue to burn and consume us. We can experience peace, joy and freedom, but they do not come through gaining more knowledge, changing our thinking, or creating new behaviors. We need transformed hearts that allow us to trust, fresh eyes to experience the beauty that grows amid the carnage, and a hunger to taste what is being offered to us. These things come from God alone—that same God we are raging against.

We will set out on this pilgrimage by surveying the very place we start. Part I, A Hemorrhaging Faith, explores both the pain and spiritual space of our anger at God. We will encounter difficult truths about what our anger contains as well the places we have dwelled. We will find a definition of our anger that is big enough for both our faith and suffering. While we long to reach the beauty of the relational horizon we see before us, we cannot rush past the soil we have been inhabiting.

In part II, The Story of Our Anger at God, we put one foot in front of the other as we stumble through the grief, spiritual anemia, old stories, and disorder affections making up our anger at God. What we find are the valleys and scorched earth of our lives. We

Introduction

find ourselves confronted by the long story behind our bitterness toward the God we once claimed to be holy and good. These are the shadows of death we simultaneously hide inside and avoided. It will become difficult to see the beautiful horizon during this stretch of our spiritual travel. For most of us, our past stories are the places we fight hard to avoid and forget. But as our feet touch this fertile ground again, we will begin to process and explore our hearts more than ever before.

After clawing our way up from dark valleys, we are accosted again by the grandeur of the glorious horizon we seek. In part III, The Story of an Abandoned God, God unfolds himself before our eyes. We are more than arrested by the difficult position where Jesus puts us and our anger. We begin to hear of God's own suffering, loss, and abandonment. With our eyes fixed on the God Jesus reveals, we begin to feel the shallowness of the portrait we paint of the false god against whom we have been shaking our fists. Just as we find out more about ourselves on this journey, we begin again to see the God we once passionately trusted and adored. It is here where we come to a fork in our path. What will we do with God and our anger now that joy, peace, and freedom can be felt and tasted?

By the time we reach part IV, Finding Our Story and Place, we are surrounded by the once distant horizon. We find the beauty to be the relationship with God given to us by Jesus. It becomes painfully clear that this spiritual journey is not over. However, we also feel trust replacing some of our skepticism. It is here we can breathe easier, let our guard down further, and begin to rest inside a relationship with a gracious and sacrificing God.

In truth, this book is only a small part of a journey that will span our entire lives. There are questions that will not be answered in these pages because God has not answered them yet. I hope that this book provides helpful signposts and ideas for the pilgrimage God calls us to take. Be careful not to turn these chapters into cemented rules to be followed. There is more mystery and paradox in this broken world than can be explained in the here and now. We have claimed to understand more than we can, and we have hardened ourselves more than we should. But mystery is not without truth, and paradox not without stability. For far too long, we have been too angry and exhausted to wrestle with God. But now is the time to begin again.

One more word of advice. This book is not for the hospital bedside or funeral gatherings. A book cannot replace the physical presence of those who love us. And this book is not a bandage for the fresh trauma of those who need time and professional care. This book cannot replace the grief needed by those who have lost important people and things. But, I hope, in time this book will offer suffering people clarity and comfort.

Also, this book is largely silent on the necessary role of community and service. This is because I find most angry believers to be distrusting and isolated. So I have tried to meet you where you are. That said, serving others and cultivating deep relationships are the best ways we get outside ourselves and offer to others the healing given to us. It is a calling all believers must answer. This calling is not something we should set aside as we face our anger at God. Our story has been given to us to share with others for their sakes. Since other authors have written extensively on this, I have instead concentrated on what God does for our personal sakes. Most of us need to spend time focusing here for a while. But our personal journey is not isolated from or at the expense of others. And we will always find our steps coming up short if they never lead us toward the poor and broken. But for now, we need to see just how broken we are ourselves.

Part I

A Hemorrhaging Faith

Chapter 1

More than We Know

AS SHE DRIVES AWAY, I hear myself say, "Why are you letting this happen to me again?" It will be years before I understand why someone important leaving feels familiar, why I say "again" as she leaves. But right now, all I feel is pain. No one gets married expecting to be divorced within two years. No one thinks about getting divorced at all. I stand there not knowing what to do. Do I keep wearing my wedding ring, or should I throw it toward the heavens that remain silent? I don't know how to move from the very place I stand, much less how to move on. Somewhere amid all my questions, I feel a rage begin to ache. Why is God letting this happen to me? Where is he?

Being angry at God might be the loneliest place a person can be. We still believe God exists. We still believe he is somehow who we need the most. And yet, we now want nothing to do with him. Now when we think about him, every ounce of our being stiffens. If our hearts had hands, they would be clinched, ready to throw a punch. Is there a more isolated place than feeling God has walked away from you? We don't have all the words needed to describe the situation, but we seem to know that God deserves our anger. We feel resolute but altogether confused. Paralyzed but ready to fight. Full of questions but shouting demands.

There is something about anger that narrows and hardens us. We see everything as either black or white. Right or wrong. There

3

is no room for ambiguity or paradox. The pain we feel is real, and something must be done about it. Whatever questions we have pale in comparison to how assured we are about our "right-ness." We are right to feel how we feel. We are right to act the way we are acting. This felt right-ness is confusing when God is the one in our angry crosshairs.

But what if there is more to the story? What if being angry at God is only the blinding glare bouncing off things inside us? What if there is more pain, more to us, more to God, and many more of us angry travelers than we know?

More Pain

It is torturous describing the pain tangled within our anger at God. Is it being stabbed in the heart, or death by one thousand cuts? Is it being smashed and flattened, or stretched and ripped apart? Burned, or frozen out? Imprisoned, or exiled? Maybe it's all of these rolled into one tangled ball of confusion and confinement. It is hard to explain to others because we ourselves cannot fully understand. How do believers in Jesus Christ find themselves raging against God? Despite all of our questions, we know one fact: we cannot stop being angry at God.

But where does the pain come from? God let us down when we most needed him. God let someone die as we prayed for her recovery. People who promised to stay left as God sat on his hands. Our reasons are as numerous as they are personal. But the common thread is God's action or inaction when we most needed him. He should have been better for us, or gotten things right. We are in pain because he let us down in the worst possible way: he isn't the God we hear him claim to be.

We usually say it in different ways: "Why would God let this happen?" "Where was God when I needed him?" "What possible good can he bring from this tragedy?" It's hard to blame us for asking such questions when we suffer. And we are suffering more than we know. We can't see it right now, but we have been suffering for a long time. Whatever the event (death, broken relationship, cancer, autism), it is just the latest pain in a long line of suffering, both big and small, finally caving in on us. Our anger feels so singularly focused, but we will be surprised to find it bleeding out from places inside us where we have not visited in a long time.

The instance of suffering making us angry with God might be the biggest and most painful one of them all, but it is not the first time we tasted the heavy hand of hurt. Wounds have a way of piling up, even for the most forgiving and devout believers. Pain informs pain just as receiving praise enforces behavior. Our suffering tells us a story. Our anger at God finds its home in our suffering, past and present. We have even more pain and sorrow inside us than we realize. Our pain has deeper roots than the present suffering we are facing. While our anger at God is sharp, it is only the tip of what bludgeons us.

More to Us

Our anger at God consumes. It taints everything. It touches every relationship we have. And it pursues us into all that we do. Because we cannot shake our need for him, our anger at God seeps out of us as we walk through our days. Our anger becomes the currency we use in the marketplace of our relationship with God. There is more of our personal beings involved in our anger than we know.

We might think our anger can be compartmentalized, but it can't. We might even think anger is somehow a purely intellectual response. But anger is a "full person" action. Our anger can be felt in our fatigued bodies as much as it resounds in our words. There is always a deeper part of ourselves in emotions that can go unseen. Our anger at God is no different. A deeper and more honest part of us is found in our anger at the God we once praised as our truest need and desire. This honest part of us doesn't always get to breathe when we are around others. We are even unaware of how we keep it hidden from ourselves. But pain has a habit of squeezing our truest selves out from behind the veneer we use to hide. As

Part I: A Hemorrhaging Faith

awful as our suffering is (and as much as it might not be our fault), our anger comes from inside us and not the events of our pain. We never thought we would be angry at God when we first responded to him in faith. Our anger shines a light on places inside us we never knew existed. We know less about ourselves than we think, even though our anger hardens our opinions about our rightness.

And in a strange way, our anger at God reveals something about him inside us. At the beginning of all things, God put something of himself inside mankind. And from Adam and Eve on, the image of God bounces around inside us as we pinball from one life event to the next. Our emotions might be tainted by sin, but they still reveal something of God in us. Our anger, in a strange way, is our attempt to live out of the image in which we are created. Said another way:

> The goal to evade anguish is undesirable because our dark emotions have a redemptive side (although this fact does not make them any less painful). Though tainted in our expression of them, they nonetheless reflect the character of God. They have the power to vocalize our deepest cry—and when that cry is uttered before God, our hearts are exposed and transformed as we glimpse his heart for us.[1]

Could we actually be trying (albeit imperfectly) to be angry at what God gets angry about? Confused as we might be, we know our motives and emotions are not as pure as God's. But we cannot shake how true our anger at him feels.

Anger is a secondary emotion that comes from the deeper waters of our soul. Those waters are filled with memories, hurts, fears, and beliefs to which we rarely pay attention. But these waters are as true about us as our need to breathe air. We might think our emotions can have no deeper meaning past their surface, but what might we find if we swim down into them? Who will we find if we look behind our anger at God? Answering that question will be as important as seeing there is more to God than we know.

---

1. Allender and Longman, *Cry of the Soul*, ch. 17.

More to God

We know that there is more to God than we see. But we never imagined that he would be a God who fails us. When we considered God's mysteries, we never thought we would find pain and loneliness for ourselves. But even as we burn in anger against him, we still hope that we don't know the whole story. But it's hard to hope when you are in such pain.

There is more to God than we know. It's a simple thing to say. We are finite creatures, and he is an infinite creator of universes. Of course we don't know everything about him. But what if our anger is just as limited as any other knowledge of him? We scream a lot of things about God in our rage. We make big assumptions about his character and worth because of pain's presence. Our "where," "what," and "why" questions are full of these assumptions. But how did we come to these assumptions? One step at a time.

For now, it's hard enough to accept how little we know about God. We need an openness to the idea that, even in the face of the pain we think God gives us, there is more to him than we see. Is there a way to be honest about both our suffering and our God at the same time? Can our suffering and God's goodness be true at the same time? That's only possible if we can both be angry at and in love with God at the same. The "God-angry" believer is just that: a true believer of God who is angry at him; no less a believer and no less angry. As much as we need to see ourselves more clearly, so too God. There is more to God than our anger and pain let us see. We are face to face with the paradoxes and tensions generations of believers have wrestled to understand. Our pain makes everything feel urgent, but there is no fast track to healing what ails us. Our pain hardens us toward an idea that we know more than we actually do.

More Travelers

Our anger feels lonely. We feel left out in the cold somehow. As we look around during Sunday worship gatherings, we are certain we are adrift on a solitary life raft. Everyone happily sings the songs and nods in agreement during the sermons. It's hard not to feel like a stranger during the required small talk after the last prayer.

If suffering is a fact of life in this fallen world, then we cannot be alone on this sea. There are more God-angry believers than we can imagine. We are not solitary travelers on this journey. While our stories are different, our hurts and confusions are the same. I am always surprised by how many people identify with my anger against our God. They never talk in large groups, but after cornering me somewhere, people confess to their fists shaking toward the heavens. We might burn in solitary confinement, but we are not the only burning temples of God.

Convincing ourselves that we are the only believers weak enough to be angry at God keeps us from living a relational life. We become more isolated and lonely. We wall ourselves off from God and his followers. Where do we have left to go other than to cave in on ourselves? We keep tumbling over our anger and pain. But we do so separated from those we most need. Because our anger involves our most precious and vulnerable wounds, we keep them hidden. But it's hard to travel in the dark without light. It feels like a great risk, especially in a church culture with little room for those stuck and helpless. But we need to step out into the light. Traveling out of our anger starts with an honest confession. We will find more angry travelers than we thought.

Anger at God sounds like strong statements and proclamations. But, the truth is, anger at God is filled with painful questions we feel he leaves us to answer on our own. If we listen, which we rarely do, we will hear "why," "what," and "where" bleeding out of us more than proclamations of certainty. Our questions point to a tension sufferers carry thousands of miles every day. We are certain of our pain, but don't know what to do with it. We know we don't have the whole story, but we try to fill in the gaps for ourselves. The picture is blurry because of our tears, but we keep assuring ourselves of what we see.

If you have picked up this book, you are beginning to step out of the denial of your anger at God. Most of us feel we only have three options when dealing with difficult emotions: denial, evasion, or fight. Most of us have been denying the anger we feel toward God. We don't like the idea of being angry with the God who hears our worship songs. And we hate the looks we get from others when the anger slips past our defenses and sees the public light of our relationships. Denial only hinders and deepens the pain.

Evasion can feel like denial in action. But it goes further. We might acknowledge our anger toward God, but through willpower and busying ourselves, we evade its reality by attempting to create a new reality with good Christian disciplines. Sometimes these disciplines are just a game we are attempting to win. But another Bible study never does the trick. Or as the great Dr. Seuss tells us, sometimes the loneliest games are the ones we play against ourselves.[2] It's devastating to realize how many of our church activities are our best attempts to run away from our hearts. We use Bible studies, group devotionals, and even Sunday worship gatherings as ways of detaching and hiding from the rage we feel toward the God who let us down.

Others of us attempt to fight both God and ourselves. We fight ourselves by placing guilt and shame upon our heads. We beat up ourselves for being "stupid enough" to believe we could actually be angry at God. Other times we fight against God, believing he has entered into a conflict against us. We believe our suffering is God's way of bringing this fight to us. It's frightening to believe God opens up his holy arsenal against us. Because we see ourselves being in conflict against God (and God in conflict against us), our anger with him grows stronger.

But we have a different option. One that refuses denial, evasion, or combat. It is turning to see the true conflict God is fighting. Turning to face the true conflict of our suffering is letting our faces be warmed by a greater reality found in God's own story. In this story we see God locked in a fight with suffering and death itself, not us. We begin to see more truths about ourselves than we ever knew. And we also see more of God than our hearts ever grasped. The rest of this book is our attempt to turn and face a conflict we have a difficult time understanding.

2. Dr. Seuss, *Oh, the Places You'll Go*, 33.

Part I: A Hemorrhaging Faith

Being angry at God won't end because we work hard to "just stop it," as some have scolded. And we certainly won't see our anger toward God dissipate because we read a book such as this. But we are not doomed to fume against God for the rest of our days. Despite what some preachers and counselors might tells us, this takes more time than we are comfortable admitting. A sermon about how Christians should be joyful and faithful won't snap us out of our anger. Four quick sessions in a counselor's office and a handful of memorized scriptures won't do the trick either. In any case, "the study of a map never replaces the 'experience' of the country itself."[3] And just like hiking, you only meet the other side of the trail when you have walked its path.

Journeying out of anger at God is a long trail full of familiar sights and sounds. It is a trail we must travel through our personal history, listening to old tales of our family and faith. Our travel forces us to climb high vistas we cannot reach without naming pain. The journey falls into low valleys as we hear lies we never knew we believed. Despite what some tell us (or we tell ourselves), our story matters. Our journey has eternal significance. It is personal. Let others watch if they want, but we don't have to listen to their critiques anymore. There will be enough for us to focus on as we make this messy journey without processing any shame others might give us for not moving the "right way" or fast enough. It takes time. Fortunately, all we have to do is put one foot in front of the other. There are no "five easy steps," but there is a way out of our anger at God that leads back to Jesus. But right now, most of us don't want to talk about Jesus because we are too angry with God. So let's talk about our story.

---

3. Rohr and Ebert, *Enneagram*, 4

Chapter 2

We Made a Home

JUSTIN SAT STUNNED. HIS counselor asked him if he was angry at God. "Why would I be angry at God? I'm angry at my parents for abandoning me," Justin responded. "Doesn't God decide the boundaries and days of your life?" his counselor bounced back. "Yeah, but that doesn't mean I *have* to be mad at him for my parents' actions," Justin shot back. "What happens in our relationships with others flows from our relationship with our Heavenly Father," the counselor continued. Feeling his lips tighten at the words "Heavenly Father," Justin recognized his anger at God for the first time. He knew he was an angry man, but he never thought his anger ran all the way up to the penthouse of heaven.

Most of us point to a specific moment when our anger at God began, a precipitating event of intense suffering or loss that birthed our anger. There is hurt we resent having, but we cannot stop feeling it. It's a repulsive smell of pain that intrudes, breeding the taste of agony we are forced to endure. It's the moment when God let us down, and now he deserves our anger. A parent slowly dies from cancer. A spouse cheats on us. A friend breaks our confidence in the most public of ways. We lose a job when our bank account is already empty. God refuses to answer our questions, so we rage further. It's hard to suffer without trying to find someone or something to blame. And God is always an easy target for us.

Part I: A Hemorrhaging Faith

But what if the so-called precipitating event was just the latest event, the straw that broke the camel's back? It's a long jump to make from praising God to raging against him. Believers can't make that leap in a single bound. What if, all along, we have been closer to our anger than we noticed?

Short Trip to the Mailbox

We live inside an involved confusion. Our anger shows us things we never thought capable of ourselves. There are many contributors to our confusion, but anger's beginning is the most pressing. Attempting to describe and explain our anger at God, we rehearse our questions about "why" and "what," but they never seem to capture the full story. It is more than a simple need to be heard that keeps us retelling our story of suffering and God letting us down. As Paul Tripp points out, we are interpretive beings.[1] We don't just experience events: we are wired to understand what is happening to us. We want to know where our pain comes from, and why it came to us at all. We look at the facts we experience, and the first moments where we notice our anger boiling against God is where we assume it starts. But anyone who has boiled water knows a simple fact: it doesn't boil on its own. Water needs a container to hold it and some form of intense heat to raise its temperature. And more importantly, it needs time to heat up. So, too, with anger. While anger can show up in the blink of an eye, it has taken more time to develop than we know. The reason anger comes to the surface so quickly is because it is not the deepest emotion or belief inside us.

As we noticed in the last chapter, anger is a secondary emotion fueled by more basic emotions and beliefs about the world we try to interpret. Even without identifying these emotions right now, we see how our anger at God started long before our suffering that pushes us to scream toward the silent heavens. Our anger at God seems to come out of us suddenly when pain is squeezing

---

1. Tripp, *Instruments in the Redeemer's Hands*, 41.

We Made a Home

tightly. But our anger travels a long way from inside us, maturing before it bursts onto the scene.

Any time I try explaining to pastors or friends my anger toward God, I get a judgmental response that sounds like, "Just stop it." They treat my anger as if I simply made a wrong emotional or theological turn over the railroad tracks into the wrong side of town. I feel minimized or dismissed. If anger at God is a simple wrong turn made into the scary part of town, then all I have to do is turn back the other direction. But my world is spinning, and I have no idea where to go. Simple devotional time doesn't help. Prayer ends in pain and silence. Reading Scripture sounds like listening to Charlie Brown's teacher.

All of this work to get back on the right side of some theological side of town just makes things worse. Now I have more prayers where God remains silent. Scripture feels irrelevant to my suffering. Church gatherings feel like being pelted with rocks by a parade of people who think I lack enough faith. I have come to understand one clear thing about my anger with God: all of my emotional and spiritual mail is delivered to an angry home address.

God-angry believers don't make a *single* wrong turn over some emotional railroad tracks into the wrong side of town. Instead, anger at God is unknowingly making a home in a scary neighborhood you never even wished to visit. Now we are surprised walking out our front door to see the brokenness and heartache around us. We crossed the tracks long ago, made many different turns, and then planted deep roots. This is not a misguided day trip. We are not renting a room. We own the property and built ourselves a place to call home. We have lived through experiences and fostered beliefs that come to house our anger at God. For many of us, we spend a lifetime growing up and making our home in places that plant and nurture the seeds of what becomes our anger at God. Like parcels that have been filtered and sorted, our emotional and spiritual "mail" is delivered to this angry address.

Only when we have new eyes to see the place where we made our home will some of our confusion lift. Again, there is nothing instant about our anger at God, and there is no quick fix either. It's

Part I: A Hemorrhaging Faith

hard to leave home, even one you can't wait to flee. Boxes need to be packed (or unpacked and left behind). And we need to find a new place to live. But even when we leave one place for another, our hearts have a tendency to find their way back to the places we knew for so long.

A Long Way Back

Some of the confusion comes from the oddly historic feeling of our freshly boiled anger. We can't shake how familiar some of our pain feels; maybe we even expected it. But once we see how we unknowingly made a home in our anger at God, our eyes begin to adjust, like when we walk out of a dark tunnel into the light. We begin to see how far back our anger at God goes. We might not yet see all of the details, but there is something helpful about seeing the contours and depth of this emotional landscape.

Before we can focus on any certain details about our anger at God, we need our eyes to adjust to the view we already see. Our anger at God reaches farther back into our story than we know. When it comes to pain and sorrow, we believe we can contain and compartmentalize ourselves. This gives us the illusion that pain doesn't instruct pain. We think past abuse doesn't influence other relationships, like hoping abandonment by an absent father won't spoil our relationships with other key men in our lives. But we do not live in a vacuum. The wounds we receive seep into the plots of the different stories we live. God made us to be fully connected with our story and connected to others. We rob ourselves of more than we save when we try walling off the painful places in our stories. We even shortchange ourselves by thinking we haven't been forming beliefs about ourselves, God, and this world. Anger is a secondary emotion that flows from beliefs, desires, and emotions forming themselves inside our stories. The details are fuzzy, but the landscape is coming into focus.

Our story is full of moments, big and small, which we harvest for meaning and guidance. Some of the smaller moments go unexamined for a long time. We don't notice a pebble on the ground until it ends up in our shoe. Other moments are so big we cannot help but notice how they shape us. Like a tree root changing the path we walk, some things alter the way we live in obvious ways. These bigger moments are hardest for our faith. It takes us longer, often in many small stages, to trust others with these difficult moments. So they stick around longer, continuing to shape how we live our lives.

All of these moments pile up and collect themselves in our souls. We experience them over and over again as we live more life. We try to create systems of understanding and categorize them in a desperate attempt to make sense of life. They inform beliefs that reach into new experiences and relationships we find.

At this point don't try to focus on the details of your anger at God yet; just notice the contours stretching back into the history of your life. We want to rush along the path of healing and peace, but rushing can lead to more pain and anxiety. Are you sensing that there might be more in your anger than just the pain? Maybe there is a story being told? A belief? A life?

Deep Roots

Our anger at God also has deep and ancient roots. Most of us God-angry people are surprised that we have been angry at him for so long. But, at the same time, most of us hold to some theological idea of "original sin." We see ourselves, to some degree, participating or being born into Adam's original sin in the garden. There is something about Adam that lives in us. It is here that most of us rush to the question: Is it a sin to be angry at God? But I'm not sure that is most helpful question for us to ask right now. Most of us are ready to fight for our right to be angry at God. But what if we ask ourselves a different question: Does all humanity have an intrinsic distrust of God?

We distrust what we do not understand. It's not always helpful, but it is part of the nature we share. Is there anything further beyond our understanding than God? Anything more confusing and at times terrifying than a God who claims to be perfect and yet personal? It's not surprising that we find ourselves angry at God. It is an outworking of our distrust of a God who tells us we will never fully understand him. But somewhere our distrust of God collided with an experience and revelation of God that overwhelmed us. Faith bloomed, and then our distrust of him waned. But faith doesn't grow in a vacuum either.

Faith grows alongside sorrow. Faith is a slow process that shares space in our lives with the decay and death of this broken world. Growing in faith is the gradual turn from distrust to trust in God. It isn't consistent or scheduled. It feels like faith starts and stops as much as it charges forward. And it's never more difficult to trust God than when our suffering seems to choke the life out of everything good we have. There is never a more difficult time to trust God with your life than when he seems to mishandle your affairs. Is he trustworthy with your soul when a parent's heart stops beating? Will he bring you good when he allows such bad things to happen in this world? Can you trust him to stay when he keeps taking people and things away? It's a long jump from praising God to raging against him. But, it's a small step from distrust to anger while in the presence of pain and injustice.

We are all people of desire. We have desires we want to be met. Desires are not bad in and of themselves. Neither are the objects of those desires in and of themselves wrong. But when our desires go unmet, anger tends to follow. We desire our children to grow healthy, but instead they get sick. A good desire goes unmet, and anger grows from deep roots. Our distrust of God is remembered, and now our unmet desire for a good thing becomes the fuel for our anger. Unmet desires tangle with pain and sorrow until we are bound in chains.

Most of us don't care about Adam or any implications of original sin right now. We are in agony, and it feels more valid to us than any theological principle. We are angry at how God lets us experience such suffering and abandonment. We thought he would protect us, but he didn't. We thought he would keep someone alive, but he didn't. When we cry out, we aren't looking for a systematic theology course. We are looking for God to comfort and heal. But he doesn't seem to be doing much of either. People we love got taken from us. Our health continues to fail as we pray with our remaining strength. We are still abandoned by those who promised to stay. God even seems to have broken his promise to never leave. Our children get violated by someone we thought we could trust. Our desires are unmet for sure. And our anger feels like the right response to God's handling of things. These angry roots might run deep, but we don't care where they lead right now. We are crumbling under the weight of pain. And all that "God's people" can seem tell us is to stop being angry and start being joyful. It's a close contest between who is more infuriating: a God who distantly hurts us, or his followers who keep shoving disjointed Bible verses into our wounds.

Close, Long & Deep

Our anger at God has been our home longer than we realize. The foundation of our anger at God starts in unnoticed moments that harden into beliefs about him. This foundation is as deep and powerful as the root system of a giant tree. Our anger at God comes from confusion and pain, and grows into more pain and confusion as we try to understand why we feel what we feel toward God. It's hard not to mix metaphors when explaining our anger because it invades so many different areas of our lives. You can't talk about your relationships the same way you talk about going to work. You can't talk about singing the same way you talk about paying hospital bills. But all of these things are affected by our anger at God. So the confusion rolls on as we reach for any metaphor we think will help us make sense of how both deep and shallow we feel in our anger. How thin but bloated we feel. How tired but enraged. Confused but resolute. Foggy but sunburnt. Consumed but alone. But we must come to a place where we can accept who we are at this moment. While we are looking for a way to journey forward, we do so acknowledging that we cannot be anywhere other than we are right now.

Part I: A Hemorrhaging Faith

So what does all this mean? If our anger at God is older than we know, where did it begin? If we truly have been living in a home built for and by our anger at God, what was used to make such a structure? If we are angry over unmet desires that are not wrong in and of themselves, why does our anger at God have a nagging feeling of guilt? If God is who he says he is, then where is he in all of this? Why is there such pain in our anger at God?

Chapter 3

What Is Our Anger at God?

I wasn't sure how much he already had to drink, but he was about to drain his glass. Ross wanted to talk, but had few words. He began fumbling through the story. His wife walked out on the family Christmas Day years ago. She left him to raise the kids on his own. He always works at least two jobs to try and make the ends meet. Ross is a perpetually exhausted father. But he lost his highest paying job this week.

"Why is God letting all this happen to me and the kids?" Ross asked as he stared at the ground. "Wasn't the abandonment enough? Why am I losing my job? What is he doing? Doesn't he know how much harder this will make things for my kids?" His questions spewed out, one after the other. Years of anger and confusion now flowed unrestrained into his empty glass. I had no words to defend God, so I drank and listened. But I couldn't help wondering why God would continue to make life so difficult for this man. He was doing his best to be a father and provide. Why was God piling more on his shoulders?

Understanding our anger at God begins with finding a definition big enough to hold the collision between our faith and sorrow. How we define our anger at God cannot shortchange either our faith in him or the pain and loss we have experienced. Without such a definition, our confusion will continue and our bitterness will only intensify. We will continue being tortured by pain and disappointment that taints every relationship we have. Joining worship gatherings will only add fuel to the fire. And our relationship with God will remain distressed. So what definition can do justice to our faith and suffering?

Anger at God is a demand for justice and God's accountability, both driven by a tapestry of grief, spiritual anemia, moral actions, and disordered affections. These four parts of our stories both arise from and affirm the experiences and beliefs fueling our anger at God. Our anger is the culmination of our search for justice in light of what we perceive as injustices. These four aspects become the force and currency of our anger. Until we understand them, we will be perpetually, to one degree or another, seeking to hold God accountable for the injustices and suffering in our lives. There will be little room in our relationship with him that feels peaceful or restful. There will only be bitter longing for something we feel has been intentionally placed out of our reach.

Grief

We are aware of our pain and suffering. They are what we recount when asked why we are angry. We are angry because God let someone die, disease ravage our bodies, lovers abandon, abuse occur, and so much more. God and his followers seem to want us to quickly move through our suffering without breaking down on the wrong side of the emotional tracks. It feels like we are alone for much of the pain we feel. It feels like God is keeping his distance because he knows he failed us. But this is just the description of the misery received. We rarely spend time processing our grief.

Grief is more than a list of our pain. Grief isn't a person dying: it is how our soul interacts with the death. Grief is the movement of our hearts as we experience pain. It is a slow process we often overlook while we attempt to go about our lives after tragedy strikes or disease eats away at our bodies. We easily get stuck inside grief's process without noticing. So much of our anger at God goes unnoticed because we pay little attention to our grief.

What Is Our Anger at God?

We don't want to feel the prolonged sorrow because the event of our suffering is hard enough. We don't want to sit inside sorrow's reality because we are convinced we should not feel the way we do. We are convinced we should be able to move quickly through the pain of losing someone or be "courageous" in the face of cancer. Somewhere in our lives we picked up beliefs that instruct us how to feel and act in light of our suffering. For us God-angry believers, something about these beliefs keeps us from experiencing or seeing the full breadth of our grief. We fail to see how the death of a loved one darkens every horizon of our lives. Grief confronts us like an invisible force, and we only tend to notice its symptoms.

When we fail to see and name grief, we risk an emotional cycle with few places to go other than anger and apathy toward God. Our grief is not wrong. In fact, it is the right response to the destruction and decay we are experiencing. We are in throes of a grief to which we pay little attention. We can name the event and people we are suffering through, but we do not notice how much grief our hearts struggle to process. Unprocessed grief causes past suffering to linger and attach itself to new experiences and relationships. Grief touches every aspect of our being. Grief that remains nameless and ignored fuels our anger at God. We are blinded by unacknowledged grief. It's hard to tell where our anger at God begins and our grief ends.

Spiritual Anemia

Having come this far, we are exhausted, fighting against the wind. We have been screaming and pleading for so long, but it doesn't get us very far. We are on some sort of emotional treadmill without a stop button. We run and run, but we still seem to be in the same spot.

Earlier we talked about original sin and then quickly established how we are too angry to care much about it right now. But things that go unnoticed often trap us. We are spiritually exhausted and anemic because we experience things for which we weren't created. We were not created to handle suffering and sorrow. Put

Part I: A Hemorrhaging Faith

away the ideas of "spiritual disciplines" and "sanctification" for a moment. Those are ideas of growth. Focus instead on the story the Bible starts telling in Genesis. It is a story that we have heard far too many times without it moving us.

Genesis describes a God who decides all that he has created will only be complete when he finishes creating humanity. And God cannot complete creating humanity until man has his own image. So, man is given a concept of beauty, a spiritual soul, and the ability (if not duty) to reflect the Creator to the rest of creation. There is no sin, so man has no barriers or hindrances to peace, joy, and freedom. Genesis implies that man was designed to live forever in a constant and beautiful relationship with God and the rest of creation. This is the state God designed our bodies and souls to experience: a reality that doesn't cause spiritual weariness.

When sin enters the picture, all of creation is plunged into a reality it is never meant to experience. Death and decay are the partners of sin. The post-Genesis 3 world is in need of rescue and reconciliation, in need of help to be what it was meant to be. God didn't create a world lacking the ability to be what it was meant to be. But after the fall, we are plunged into a world that wars against us. We now need to find ways to exist in a world for which we are not equipped.

Disease isn't supposed to slowly eat away our bodies. Relationships are not supposed to break down. But this is the reality we all live inside. It's exhausting trying to do something we are not equipped to do. Run a marathon without months of training, and you'll be gassed long before you see the finish line. It's the same with suffering and sorrow. At our core, we were not created to suffer.

Before we start interjecting all our theology about the Holy Spirit and progressive sanctification, we have to recognize that sin, death, and suffering have no place in God's created order. They are intruders. They rip apart and smear what should be whole and clean. And every moment we breathe, they slowly and forcefully push against us as we try to make sense of life.

Like a crowding darkness, death and pain cause us to slow down (and even stand still) as we attempt to live. But even in light

What Is Our Anger at God?

of redemption and salvation, we are faced with the undeniable truth that we cannot live this life as we should. We need someone to rescue, comfort, and even revive us. We have reached a place where we cannot go any further.

Being angry at God is a spiritual exhaustion no longer allowing us to catch our breath. We can no longer shoulder the suffering, loss, and doubt we carry. Faith feels as burdensome as the pain. We try to keep walking but feel too wounded to soldier on and fight the good fight. Right now, we are having a hard time letting the idea of a good and loving God override all the heartache and emptiness we are experiencing. Faith is an incredible weight to bear on its own. But when we try to have faith and grieve the agony of loss and sorrow, it doesn't take long to grow weary and break down. Instead of saddling ourselves with new shame in some faith comparison game, we need to see how we live in a world bent on wearing us down.

Moral Action

It's hard to explain what anger feels like. Some of us physically have a burning sensation at times. Our bodies get tense. Anger feels like a burning in our soul. Words fail to describe our anger for many reasons. But the biggest reason they fail is because we don't recognize anger as an action we take. Anger is a feeling, but it needs to be understood further.

Robert Jones explains that anger is a "whole-person" judgment we make against a perceived wrong.[1] Our anger at God is no different. Most of us don't hear what we say about God in our anger. Initially, we might be shocked at ourselves, or even feel guilty. But the more time we spend boiling and hurting, we stop caring as much. Our hurts and questions go unanswered, so our anger picks up speed. And we race past the shock and guilt. Even now, when hearing the idea that our anger is a choice we make, our hurting souls race too fast to consider the ramifications.

1. Jones, *Angry at God?*, 4

Part I: A Hemorrhaging Faith

Anger feels like a natural reaction we have when things don't go as we thought they should. The seductive and intrusive thing about anger is how "right" it feels standing in the landscape of our hurts and sufferings. We think we have a profound insight into ourselves, but honestly we don't. We have a difficult time seeing past pain and the now. Pain bullies our hearts into a corner until it consumes our thinking and seeing. Then we have trouble looking down the long history of our lives without the present hurt and anger coloring all we see and hear. We become short-sighted. In this way, we make the choice to be angry at God because the hurt and pain is all we see and feel. It is an easy choice to make in light of the grief and exhaustion, but these feelings also keep us from seeing the choice we are making.

There is so much at stake for us in our anger at God. So much hangs in a balance of a need for him that is laced with rage and grief. But if our anger is a choice we are making against God, then it is somehow not a something outside of us. Our reasons for this choice are a true part of ourselves that we no longer have the strength to hold at bay, much less deny. Our anger at God is a choice we make based on beliefs and supposed facts we have accumulated.

Our anger with God is our cry for justice in the face of his apparent inability to deliver on the promises he made to us. We are too crowded by pain and confusion to even question the seeming evidence of God's treason against us. But if we are ever going to make this journey out of our anger, we need to examine again the facts of the case we bring against God. Is it possible that we don't have all the information? Is it possible that we don't see enough of the picture of our suffering and pain? If there truly is a lot at stake in our anger at God, then we must answer these questions.

Understanding anger as a moral choice is as important as recognizing our grief and exhaustion. Our anger at God is not something that happens to us, nor is it a random reaction. It is a moral response we make in pursuit of justice based on the evidence we see against him. However, our moral choices are driven by the affections we hold tight.

What Is Our Anger at God?

Disorder Affections

Beneath the choice we each make to be angry at God, our hearts are full of competing affections. We *want* to want God more than anything, but we rarely do. Even before the suffering that supposedly started our anger at God, we had a difficult time wanting God more than what we find in this world. Affections show what we worship because we worship what we most desire. At the end of the day (and the end of our anger at God), we are constant worshipers of someone or something.

This idea can make us boil over very quickly because it puts pressure on our suffering. So let's be clear. It is not wrong to desire for God to heal or protect someone we love. It is not wrong to desire and enjoy a vocation of our choosing. It is not wrong to hope for a limited amount of suffering in our lives. These are all good desires that reflect the heart of God himself. It is shameful to tell a mother to stop grieving the death of her child. It is wicked to demand those suffering to hurry through their griefs. Friends and pastors offer counsel that sounds something like this: "Your hurt is understandable, but don't let it get the best of you. . . . Don't stay hurt too long. . . . Don't mourn the loss too much. . . . It's okay to feel sorrow for now, but not much longer." We do not have the power to control the length and depth of our griefs any more than we have the power to gain salvation through our right actions. Grief and sorrow are functions of our hearts; the same hearts we do not have the power to change. Pain and sorrow plunge into us as deep as they are going to sink. Trying to control them only increases the pain because we will inevitably choose to deny their existence or heap guilt and shame on ourselves for having them at all. Neither help.

Even still, our disappointments and anger with God point to the disordered nature of our affections, desires, and worship. In order to be angry at God, we have to make a judgment against him. This judgment points to an affection we have for something we find greater than him. When losing something or someone becomes justification for our anger at God, we have desired it more than him. If we experience a suffering or trauma that produces our anger at God, we value what is tampered with more than God. This line of thinking can feel enraging when what is lost or hurt are people we are called to love and even protect. How can it be wrong to have a high affection for our children and loved ones? How can it be wrong to value our own health? It's not, in and of itself.

Grief is the right response to suffering and loss in a world God never wanted decay and death to enter. Our grief actually reflects the very heart of God. But when grief is mixed with our spiritual anemia and exhaustion, we begin to see a clear picture of our hearts. If our spiritual exhaustion points to our lack of endurance to weather the storm of this fallen world, then we inevitably begin to see signs of our disorder affections. The question "If (blank) were taken away, but God remains, would he be enough?" is a simple hypothetical question to answer for good church folk. That is, until whatever it is that fills in the blank is actually taken away or damaged. Life is too complicated for such a simple question, but the way we live out the answer is telling. Where we respond in anger and disappointment with God, we find the places God is not enough for us. We find things we value and desire more than him.

But where do we draw the line between too much affection and just enough affection? How much is too much when it comes to loving and protecting your children? How about our spouses? Our jobs? Our health? We don't know the answers to those questions until these things are threatened or taken away. But our anger at God is a sure sign we love and cherish something more than him. Even the most watchful and disciplined believer has disordered affections when it comes to God. Having disordered affections—which lead to wrongfully directed worship—is the reality of all of our hearts in a post-Genesis 3 world. The faith that slowly grows in the midst of our sorrow and pain is a process just like grief. Both reveal things about our hearts we could not see before. But our anger at God has a way of blinding us to what is being revealed, and even hardening our hearts. A hard heart leaves little room for others. But room, more than anything, is what we God-angry believers need.

Making Room

We have a limited understanding of our personal histories. But this personal history shapes our hearts, molding and orienting our beliefs and desires. And we need to come to terms with the idea that we have been forming and progressing in our anger at God longer than we realize. We have made a home in our anger toward him, not some wrong turn that can be easily corrected. Without noticing it, our experiences have been filtered and processed through beliefs and assumptions that build the foundation for our anger. Our anger at God is the fruit being nourished by these deep foundational roots. These are truths that have to be acknowledged if we are ever going to make our way out of our anger at God.

We must see how our anger at God is a demand for justice and God's accountability driven by a tapestry of our grief, spiritual anemia, moral actions, and disordered affections. These four parts of our story both rise from and strengthen the beliefs leading to our anger at God. As hard as it is, we need to enter more deeply into our grief. Grief is fertile soil for our anger at God. Our grief is not wrong. But what we do with that grief sheds light into the deeper caverns of our hearts. We begin to see just how exhausted we are from trying to live in a world pushing against us. We need to come to terms with the choice we make to be angry at God based on our quests for personal justice. And we will begin to see how little we desire God in comparison to the things suffering and sorrow threaten to take from us. All of these aspects of our anger at God weave themselves together. Focusing on one at the exclusion of the rest, we will either feel personally justified or unpardonably shamed. Neither of these paint a picture of how God sees us. The rest of our journey out of our anger at God is a slow process of making room to see and experience great truths about ourselves and God. We will look more closely at all four aspects of our anger at God.

The picture we paint of God with our words and beliefs is one who deserves our anger. Even the most angry believer knows that he needs a better picture of God. We also have a skewed picture of ourselves. There is more to us than we see, and the lives we

Part I: A Hemorrhaging Faith

experience have more meaning than most of us care to know. So we need to see the story of our anger at God as much as we need to discover the story of an abandoned God. In the end, this will help each of us find our own story and place. But none of this is as easy as the choice we made to be angry with God.

The hardest thing for an angry person to do is to make emotional room for the presence of the other person. It is difficult to hear his side of the story. Because grief and exhaustion are such big parts of our anger at God, making room takes time. Because there are beliefs and affections tied to this anger toward God, it takes time to search and understand the depths of our heart being exposed. But making room for God is what our soul needs. Our grief and suffering need God like our lungs need air. Our history needs God to anchor it inside a greater story. Now that we have a general idea of the landscape of our anger at God, we can begin to simply place one foot in front of the other and survey the details of this trail we are walking.

Part II

The Story of Our Anger at God

Chapter 4

Frozen Grief

I didn't notice when the hurt turned into anger, but at some point the anger felt like home. Now, as I sat across from Ken, my counselor, my anger was being exposed for its power to rob me of my ability to grieve. Ken spoke softly, attempting to tread lightly on the sensitive ground turned holy through my tears. "You have not moved through your grief because it's easier to stay angry," he cautiously instructed. "Grief takes many forms traveling through many stages. But processing grief does not end with you being crushed under a collapsing cave you sought for protection."

"What is the cave I wanted to protect me? And why is it caving in on me?" I mumbled.

"You thought your anger could protect you from the long winter of abandonment," Ken offered.

"Anger is a part of the process!" I pushed.

"But it's not the end of the journey. In fact, anger can create a winter of its own . . . even when we are burning against people," he said gently, guiding me out of my crumbling cavern.

"That's doesn't make sense. Now I feel angry at myself for not understanding!" I replied.

"Your anger can't protect you from the hurt and fear. You can't run away from your history. You are frozen in grief because your bargaining with God has failed . . . and it makes you angry," he continued.

Part II: The Story of Our Anger at God

"What are you talking about?" I began to boil.

"Talking about your suffering is a good step, but it is not the end of grief. Prolonged anger, especially at God, keeps us from truly grieving. It keeps our hearts from fully interacting with the pain and loss. You are burning angry, but frozen in paralysis at the same time. You live in a paradox," he said, tying his thoughts together.

We are churning in our anger at God. We are exhausted and weak in a spiritual contest between faith and unbelief. We are frozen in our tracks and burning with rage all at once. This is the internal life of the God-angry believer. Our days are confusing and full of contradictions. We say a lot, but we hardly touch the deeper hurts of our hearts. Our anger is unbelievably consuming, and yet we are horribly undernourished. We know about suffering, but are largely estranged from the grief we need to walk through.

Most of us know something about the different "stages" of grief people walk through after losing a loved one (a process moving from denial to acceptance). But few of us see our need to grieve or the fact we keep our hearts from truly experiencing such a process. And even those of us who acknowledge our need are fooled into thinking our anger at God is the culmination of such a process. But instead, our anger at God points to suffering suspended inside hijacked grief.

Grief Processing

Our hearts need to step into the grief that has a journey of its own. Our heart needs the freedom to explore how deep the suffering reaches, and how delayed by our anger pointed at God. True grief happens through freedom. But God-angry believers do not feel such a freedom. We had the freedom once, but we chained it up when grief became more dangerous than we were comfortable exploring. Grief is movement even if it is falling flat on our face. But we have not moved for quite awhile.

Grief has a movement that might feel circular, but it is actually moving in a salient direction. It stretches both deep and high in a spiraling movement, reaching outward from inside us. It touches the deepest places of our existences while simultaneously allowing our hearts to reach higher than they once did. But we should not confuse *process* with *progress*.

We do not need ideas of progress guilting us. We often let ideas of *progressive sanctification* shut down our grieving if we aren't paying attention. And, as we have already noticed, we have not been paying attention to much more than our pain. Grief is not a process of moving from "wrong" to "right." Instead, grief is a passage from foggy pain to peace. Grief is an aspect of sanctification that allows our hearts a chance for greater rest, even if this rest does not necessarily give us all the answers we desire. However, moving out of our constant confusion is vital.

Grief is what our hearts *do* with the suffering and loss we experience. Grief is the slow healing that the entire cosmos is aching to experience. Grief is not an enemy of sanctification and restoration. When we consider the affliction and distress we have experienced at the hands of death and sorrow, grief is the right response. Grief, strictly as an idea, is a term we use to house our numbness, anger, denial, and bargaining with God; it is also the acceptance we experience in the wake of suffering's intrusion. Grief has many moving parts that refuse to stay static or play in a particular order. Grief even refuses to be numbered in a way that is universally accepted by "experts." Even still, grief's process is important for the healing of the heart. Grief is not stationary, but it can freeze due to excessive exposure to a believer's rage. The heart simmers continuously when other stages of grief (and even other steps of faith) have refused to give us a desired outcome.

Grief is not an enemy of faith. Grief is actually a movement of faith. Grief is risk. When we grieve distress and loss, we are traveling a path of trust and acceptance of God's love and care. This alone reveals why we have not grieved. We do not trust God based on his past performance. So why should we trust him now with a grieving process that ultimately wagers our most precious things on God's ability to come through? We don't trust him to handle what is fragile and most meaningful for us. We might have started to grieve until we stumbled upon the ease and pleasure of anger. There are many people and things to be angry at when grief is moving within our hearts, but none feels quite as paramount a choice as God when he seemingly refuses to hold up his end of the bargains we made with him.

Bargaining Bin

An odd stage of grief is called *bargaining*. Bargaining can best be described by the phrases *promise* and *should have*. And, without always knowing, we bargain with God.

With past suffering and loss of precious things, we made some promises to God we believed he would honor with a desired response. A parent abused us, so we promised God we would not repeat whatever action or speech that caused them to harm us. We expected God to keep further abuse from happening as long as we held our ends of the bargain. But the abuse came again and again. At some point we wondered why God did not keep our agreement. Or it could be smaller instances (but not less important), such as studying harder to get good grades, or preparing tirelessly for a job interview. When the grade doesn't match our preparation or the job offer goes to someone else, we wonder if God cares about the commitment. The death of a sibling whom we promised to protect. The slow disease eating away our insides, even after we promised to live an obedient life with our remaining time. Our parents divorce in the face of our promises to be a better child. A beloved child dies in the middle of the night, even after we checked her room for monsters and gave enough covers for warmth. These are all examples of pain that inform the following grief and even future instances of pain.

Sometimes we bargain by beating ourselves up. We wail on ourselves with ideas that we should have tried harder or fought the insurance company one more time to get the procedure we think would have saved a loved one's life. But in the end, most of our bargaining and shouts of "should have" land on God's doorstep. "*You* should have saved my child because *I* did everything right in raising them!" we yell at him. Much of our bargaining is rooted in promises and agreements we believe God makes with us. If we do [fill in the blank], God will do [fill in the blank]. God will keep us safe from further abandonment if we wall ourselves off from any potentially harmful relationship. God will keep our children safe if we give them proper education, nutrition, cloth diapers, enough time on the playground, a watchful eye for potential predators, and no processed sugar! God will give me this job because I worked honorably in the job I unfairly lost. God will do because I have done. My work will make God respond favorably. But did God ever make these promises? Or are they beliefs we heard from people and places we thought spoke with God's authority?

In our grief, past or present, we bargain with God trying to make him deliver *blessings* based on our actions. It is our way of trying to keep further pain away from us. But when God doesn't keep his end of the bargain, we feel justified in our anger at him. And when God becomes the target of our anger, grief is prolonged until it freezes. We might be stomping our feet, shaking our fists, and yelling at the top of our lungs; but we have stopped moving deeper or further in grief's process. When our heart is not moved by the beauty of God, it hardens. When we think God is not trustworthy because he broke promises, we refuse our true grief. We refuse to let go of the pain. There is a difference between Jacob wrestling with God in the middle of the night and our attempt to shake some justice into God by grabbing at the lapels of his jacket. One is fighting for faith and beauty. The other is hoping to blacken the eye of the one who fails us.

We might intellectually know that we cannot bargain with God, but it doesn't stop us from trying. Especially when it comes to things most precious to us. We hedge our bets. We cautiously hand God our children, careers, friends, and spouses only after he has given us his word that he will return them to us unharmed and unchanged. After all, we have worked so hard to keep them safe and happy. Or have we been working hard to keep ourselves safe and happy? Either way, our natural tendencies to distrust God cause us to bargain and demand promises about his response to our "right actions." But when more suffering comes, as it always does, our bargaining is replaced with anger. God fails us. And, in our anger, we stand frozen as we protest his breaking of promises. We are not grieving—we are trying to punish.

Continual Collapse

When we stop grieving the pain and agony, we stop moving toward God. We stand on our own ability to make sense of the misery. We are taking it upon ourselves to find a way through the darkness of days lined with loneliness. Is there any rational explanation of the abuse a child receives from the parent who is called to protect and nurture? Is there any way to clear up the confusion of losing a job of twenty years because of cutbacks? Is there any helpful definition for a child's death after only three years of life? We can only stand alone under such weight for so long. And it doesn't take long for us to collapse on ourselves.

When suffering is not grieved, our hearts are forced to relive the misery. Since we are trying to make God pay through some type of "cosmic court case," he becomes the defendant while we play the role of prosecutor. Anger at God is a lonely place because we intentionally stand apart from his advances toward us. We distrust his words and care because his track record shows his inability to come through when we needed him the most. Standing still and alone, our ability to grieve is frozen inside by our anger at God, and we crumble in one way or another. We are unable to build new relationships because if God cannot be trusted, who can? Our current relationships wither away because our friends and families desperately try to get us to turn away from our anger at God. When we have not grieved something worthy of honest grief, we force our hearts to carry an ever-increasing weight.

A grief that has not been moving toward God will always push a responsibility onto us. When God cannot be trusted, we can only trust ourselves to protect the important people and things in our life. If one child has died because God didn't keep his promises, it is our duty to keep the other children safe. If we are abandoned because God refused to confine a spouse to their promises to us, it is left to us keep our hearts from being hurt again. If my father left without an explanation, it must be my fault for making him leave. And in the privacy of our souls, we begin to protect our ever important suffering. When we cannot trust God enough to grieve, we must protect ourselves. Especially when God is the one to blame for the injustice of our afflictions.

Our backs begin to bow until our hearts can no longer carry the weight of a life not grieved. We collapse under all the pain and the emptiness. Our hearts need to grieve, but we don't trust God with such precious parts of us. And now, as we exhaustedly gasp for air underneath the rubble of ourselves, we feel alone. Our faith refuses to let us believe this is where we belong, but our distrust in God questions if we have any other place to go. At least now, we begin to think, we are out of the reach of further pain and loss. Who could possibly get to us under all this wreckage? But our faith harasses even this idea. And our anger at God finds new fodder for its fire. Alone but hounded. Frozen but boiling over. Stationary but not resting. In need of peace but defenses always up. Faith and suffering grow beside one another in a tangled jungle. Refused grieving leads to our anger at God.

It's the difference between an open wound and a scar. The wound bleeds and is not healed. It keeps us from moving and traveling. It constantly needs its dressing changed. But a scar is a wound healed by the process of grief and care. The scar is present but doesn't keep us from traveling. A scar reminds us, but it does not stop us from taking risks inside our relationships. A scar always carries a sensitivity to harsh touch, but it can experience pressure without busting open the way a wound does.

God-angry believers are the walking wounded. We are bleeding out from gashes not healed through the grieving process. We are losing life as we refuse to move through our anger. We continue to confuse medicine for danger, even confusing the doctor for a perpetrating enemy. New sufferings have deepened old wounds we have unknowingly been nursing. They become a deepening cut into an old slice that won't stop bleeding into all of our

Part II: The Story of Our Anger at God

relationships. Our anger at God is proof of the frozen grief we hid away in a now-collapsing cave of ourselves. Pain informs pain.

Old wounds create the currency we exchange inside the lives we now lead, steered by hurt and fear. We hate the hurts and loathe our fears. We would rather be angry than face these scary parts of ourselves. We are afraid they are the truest parts of us when we are dying to be brave, loving, and worthy. We desire to move on but reject the opportunities to trust and honestly grieve. We want more yet refuse to journey into the risk of losing what has become normal.

If we are angry at God, we are refusing to grieve. True grieving is a process of increasingly learning to turn to God with the unexplainable things of a world broken by death and decay. Conversely, anger at God is actively distrusting him. While anger is assuredly part of grief's process, anger at God is our refusal to risk trusting him. We have every right to be angry that death and decay are a reality in our lives. God himself burns with such anger. But being angry at God is not being angry with what God is angry at.

We have a lot of grieving to do. We might have confused our anger at God with grief, but we need to feel the difference. I am not sure that there is a *right way* to grieve. Many of us refuse to grieve because we believe we should "be better" or have "more faith." We fail to see just how big of a loss we have experienced. But whatever the reasons, we need to see that grief is the right response to the throes of agony and displacement.

Our journey out of anger at God requires *honest travel*. We have to name our suffering for what it is. We have to inventory what we have lost. If we are going to put one foot in front of the other, we have to examine and catalog where we step. We are in a dark valley of unnamed or untended suffering. We have to walk slowly and name what we see. Experiencing an absent parent is suffering that extends itself into future relationships. Call it what it is, and take the risk of grieving the pain and loss. It is a weight you have been carrying too long. The loss of a child cannot be repaired by pouring yourself into another. Don't fight the grief, because grieving is what such a loss deserves. Whatever you find in this valley of sorrow, name it for what it is. Name it, and allow yourself to grieve.

Caution

We will hate how long grief takes, but it won't be rushed just because we have places to go. It's true that we have lives we must continue, but grief is a process we can take with us. In fact, it will refuse to stay at home while you go to work or take a vacation. But acknowledging what we are carrying changes how we travel. The heavier the load, the smaller the steps we will take. We will stop hurting ourselves by trying to run when we only have strength to shuffle. Grief means trusting a God with whom we have become suspicious. This suspicion, as we have already seen, will make it almost impossible to grieve. But as we will see, such distrust is based on both lies and "secondhand truths" we have accumulated. They are another piece of this tapestry we experience as anger at God. Spiritually exhausted from suffering and loss, we refuse to grieve because being angry with God is a shorter trip in interpreting the unexplainable pain and distress.

Our suffering is the place we most need God to meet us. To care for and heal us. Our grieving is the place where God wants to meet and hold us. To grieve our suffering with us. To speak softly to us. But we are running away from the place where he is waiting to meet us. And all the while we are wondering where he is. Yet he is in our grieving. We still might not want to hear about God and what he wants, but it doesn't change that we know where to find him. He can always be found tending to our wounds, even if we are refusing his care. We want to flee from grief while God wants to carry us through it.

There will be places in this journey we can go no further until we believe and trust certain truths. But this valley of sorrow and unprocessed grief is not one of them. For some of us, we need to stay here a long while. We need to search and cry because we have avoided both for so long. It is right and good for us feel the weight of a life that has been miscarried and lost. None of us should rush where grief calls us to slow down.

Others of us have visited this valley before and already cataloged so much of the suffering found. There are only a few new

Part II: The Story of Our Anger at God

things that have grown since our last visit. We only need to refresh our memories, taking notice of new things attaching themselves to old things. Maybe we have learned how to carry grief with us as we go, but have only recently come to observe we are carrying more weight than we originally packed. The amount of time grief takes should not determine our willingness to enter into the process. But we should not feel a demand to find suffering that is not present.

We do not need to hurt ourselves with a morbid introspection that squeezes all of our life into a valley of sorrow. Find what you can here. Be honest. Name suffering and loss as you find it. If tears come, allow yourself a breakdown. Everyone is entitled to a breakdown. If tears don't come, then don't demand them. You can only be where you are! Then put one foot in front of the other as best you can. Realize this journey will take as long it will take. But don't forget there is still more ahead. You will get there when you get there.

Chapter 5

Too Tired to Think, Too Far to See

It's been over ten years since I asked God not to let someone important abandon me again. Remarried and now a father, I find myself recycling emotions and words. I am angry and hurt, but it isn't newly received wounds driving me to a counselor. After all the years, I am agonizing over the "again" I said so long ago. Surveying my life, I notice how it is littered with various amounts of suffering and loss. I have long been labeled an angry person, but few seem to help me see a larger pattern. But now, the intensity of the pain I feel begins to scare even me. There is no physical violence, but I see the emotional chaos experienced by those I most love. I am hurting and desperate. I am raging inside against God because of how much it hurts to live my life.

So as I sit in the waiting room to meet my counselor for the first time, I don't hide how broke down I feel. But I cannot remember how long I have felt this way. All I know is that I need help understanding why the latest loss of a job opportunity feels like such a massive blow and why it seems to be a familiar wound. I need help understanding all the hurt I am carrying beneath the new pain being delivered.

We are confused and hurting, but we don't entirely know why. How did we get here? Anger is a secondary emotion driven by a knotted ball of fear and hurt. If it is true that our anger at God consists of grief, spiritual exhaustion, moral action, and disordered affections, how do we untangle one from another? If all we have been able to see so far is the "general landscape" of our anger at God like a distant terrain, how will we be able to get close enough to see more of the details?

We are exhausted. Not just physically, but emotionally and spiritually. We have been running on empty longer than we think. And it didn't happen all at once. Spiritually, we have been losing fuel for quite awhile. Gradually, it becomes harder and harder to lift our heads beyond the horizon of the life we each experience. But then we cannot see as far as we think we should. And worse, we cannot imagine there being a story greater than our own. If our spiritual exhaustion and anemia comes from the weight of our suffering and grief, it is also prolonged by the length of the journey we travel. We also feel the weight of the journey we expect ourselves to continue trudging through. It becomes hard to hope or have faith with our eyes only able to see all that is broken or gone.

The Weight of Suffering

Imagine watching a weary traveller walking across a desert with a giant wooden beam balanced across his shoulders. He is buckling under the weight yet refusing to drop the beam. Feet slipping, back breaking, and running out of breath, he collapses. You can't help but wonder why he is carrying the weight. If you can image your heart somehow having shoulders, this is the picture you would see. Suffering is weighty, and our hearts do the heavy lifting.

Keep picturing the man carrying the giant wooden plank. Does he have any place other than his shoulders to carry such an odd load? Suffering is large and irregular. There is no *good way* to carry it on our journey. It is too large to be placed away in the bottom of any bags we pack. And the suffering we carry refuses to share a container filled with the other things we pick up along the way. Suffering demands more space than we have to give.

As we keep using the word "suffering," most of us continue to focus on the biggest or most recent pain we are trying to carry. But the truth is, we carry many smaller events of suffering and loss that, on their own, don't feel very bulky or heavy. However, when gathered and stockpiled, our hearts have a formidable burden. After a while, our hearts don't know where to stow away another painful piece of luggage. Some people talk about carrying the *weight of the world*, but we don't have the strength for our own individual worlds of pain, much less anyone else's. And at some point, the baggage we use rips apart and our exhausted hearts crash into an angry heap.

Some people talk about scars and wounds as souvenirs from their travels. But are our sufferings and pains prized possessions? They shouldn't be. Instead, these wounds and sufferings keep us from traveling down the roads we long to experience. There are places we hope to see, but because of our souvenirs, we are too loaded down to make such a journey. We have carried our sufferings as far as we can go, and now we are buckling under the weight. If, as we saw earlier, we are not created to carry such a load in the first place, why are we so shocked to find ourselves broke down and angry? We have been headed toward this collapse for a long time. It's not that we have just now become angry at God. We are just too exhausted to hide it anymore. The pain and loss have both become too much. Our anger is now exposed, even to ourselves.

A Thousand Miles on a Soul Worn Thin

The weight of suffering wears us thin like shoe soles walked over too many miles. Our hearts have been described by many people as the centers or seats for our persons. The heart is where all of our being is processed. Every moment we live, relationship we have, and even physical sensation we experience in some way passes through the heart. The heart travels a greater distance during our lives than we notice. Our hearts are the place where we form beliefs based on experiences. Our hearts are where our emotions, thoughts, and actions form and disperse. Our hearts are constantly trying to make sense of life. They create filters to screen each idea and physical experience that happens to us. Our hearts touch

Part II: The Story of Our Anger at God

every aspect of who we are and how we come to understand our lives—especially our sufferings.

While we can suffer physically, the hearts always take the brunt of suffering's force. If we again imagine our hearts having shoulders that carry suffering, we see our shoulders bruised and bleeding from constant exposure to heavy weight. As each of our hearts constantly interprets our lives, it makes connections between one type of suffering with another: it catalogs and organizes until the suffering has some type of meaning that can be understood and acted upon. Imagine the wear and tear our hearts go through. Our hearts orient our *true selves* more than our physical bodies ever can. We are indeed both body and soul, and one aspect of us is not better or more important. But when it comes to being angry at God, our hearts walk a longer path and feel the exposure of the harsh desert of suffering.

The longer we suffer and the more torment we experience, our hearts start roving and wandering at exhausting speeds. We are pacing to make sense of seemingly senseless things. We put our faith in God with the hope that some amount of peace and joy will be found. Perhaps some were found, but they felt more like a few drops of rain during a drought. How are we to understand the silence and distance of God when overcome by pain? Our hearts try to make sense of this new absence of God based on all we have heard and encountered in our pasts. It doesn't take long for our hearts to feel overloaded and overworked.

Eventually our hearts only have energy to travel shorter and shorter distances, returning to the past sufferings and current pain now interpreting one another. Our hearts always use the same energy, but now they collect smaller pieces of our experiences to construct stories that help us interpret our present sufferings. Our hearts have shrunk the story we see into a narrative that is bite-sized. Now we are fed only by a story that excludes so much of the lives we live. It's easy to become angry at God when the only story we are experiencing is the current and past pain of life. The moments of peace and joy we once had pale in comparison to the pain pouring over us.

It becomes even easier to question and altogether drop beliefs we once strove to follow. It doesn't take long for God's goodness to feel suspect. Much like those relationship that dealt hurtful blows to us, God becomes a perpetrator of unkept promises. Where the heart once found the hope and truth of God in the broad swath of life events, it only has the strength to travel to the closest and deepest wound at its center. Our hearts inform us of the need to protect and defend where they once called us to hope and risk. A soul worn thin by so many miles of rehearsed pain tries to find insulation and protection.

The Covering Fog

Exhausted under the weight of suffering, our hearts begin traveling less spiritual distance in order to interpret our wounds. Like a blanket of fog, our hearts begin to be hemmed in only by the suffering we have placed around them. The very real pain we experience seems to be all we see. And like headlights bouncing off fog, the suffering shines back. With the eyes of our hearts full of hurt, pain begins to interpret pain.

A parent abandoning us becomes *the* single experience informing every other relationship. The physical presence of disease begins to inform our convictions of how others must see us. The sickness of a child bends our actions toward our other children. Soon the fog surrounding our suffering insulates us from any reality other than our pain. It happens in big and small ways and goes unnoticed. No one sees the ways you eject yourself from relationships due to fear of being abandoned again. Covering your skin with long sleeves becomes your *style* instead of shielding yourself from the reaction of people getting a glimpse of the marks of disease. You become an *involved* parent as a way of fighting your fears of losing another child. Pain informs pain, suffering is continually experienced, and the fog thickens.

The longer we are trapped in this fog, the easier it becomes to disconnect from life outside. The fog perpetuates the small narrative of our lives we have come to understand as the plot of our story. But somewhere in us there is a longing for a place beyond the mist. We don't know what to call such a place, but we cannot keep ourselves from wanting to be there. The longing goes unquenched and anger begins to grow. We begin to taste the disdain we have for this confining story we stand inside. Staring at the wall of fog, we are convinced someone is at fault for the suffering and pain. We would look for the culprit, but the fog will not let us search far. So we begin to round up the most likely of suspects. While the list might grow in length, God is our main focus. If our emotions tell us something about what we are doing with the God we believe in, then we are blaming him.

Because of this fog, we are suddenly and perpetually surrounded by all the pain we can remember. Every relationship we stumble into is interpreted by the perpetually present pain we blame on God. Our exhausted hearts take our suffering and find a path to live inside a story that will help us regain some of the control and stability we think we lost in our suffering. But our hearts have not gathered together everything. Indeed our hearts have never had all of the "facts" needed to create the full story. But now it seems our hearts are too exhausted to fight through the fog. Stuck. Oppressed. Betrayed. Abandoned. Violated. And we see no reason to believe it won't happen again and again. How could God let this happen to us again?

Each of us has our own collection of suffering and pain we have lived through. It is impossible to list them all. In fact, you probably have more difficult places in your own story than you even realize. We all carry hurts and questions that never seemed to get healed and answered. Some we have carried so long that we forget they are stuffed at the bottom of our bags. But now that we have broken down in an angry mess, maybe we can look at what causes us to live so exhausted. But taking such an inventory isn't the goal in and of itself. Sometimes we can spend so much time taking inventory that we forget about the journey we need to travel. However, more times than not, most of us have not spent time inspecting what we carry. It is actually one of the reasons we are so exhausted. Most of us try to live as if we are not as hurt and wounded as we are. Our suffering is as personal as our fingerprint. The question becomes, "Do I recognize the ways I have suffered, past and present?"

Some of the pastors and friends we try to talk to seem more interested in encouraging us to admit guilt and sin than helping us to wrestle with the sufferings we experience. We get the impression that we should pay little attention to our burdens, or somehow view them as weaknesses in our faith. But we are beginning to see this as foolish. Trying to understand our anger at God without identifying and wrestling with our distress is like finishing a puzzle without every piece. We never see the entire picture of what is happening to our hearts as they carry the terrible weight of our pain.

There are many details of our hurts that must be examined on our own, but here we get a closer look at one area of the trail out of our anger at God. We are beginning to see where earth has been scorched by fire. We see withered plants choked out by harsh weather. But we are also beginning to notice small shoots growing in barren places. Could it be that even amid the thorns and thistles there is life growing around us? New life? Old life discovered? Could it be that, even as we closely examine this difficult terrain, beauty has a chance to grow? Are there places of suffering you have yet to see and name as suffering?

Walking this journey away from our anger at God demands *honest travel*. We have to be true to the terrain as we find it. Where there is unforeseen suffering, we have to be honest about where it lies in each of our journeys. Where relationships are destructive and wounding, we desperately need the honesty and courage to name them for what they are. We begin to find the fog slowly starting to lift as we get closer to the suffering we experienced, and now we intend to travel beyond the suffering. Walking through our suffering might feel like a valley of death, or it might get harder to breathe, as if climbing a tall mountain. Whatever the landscape, name it for what it is. A valley of suffering or a peak of past pain, just name it as you put one foot in front of the other. If we look around at the rest of the scenery, we see suffering is not the only

Part II: The Story of Our Anger at God

place we will go. It might feel like a never-ending forest, but the tree line will break before us sooner than we think.

Name the suffering for what it is when you find it. Explore the ways it has affected you. Try to identify the author of the suffering. And ask yourself what you have *done* with the pain. Are you trying to ignore it, acting strong when you are weak? Is there more to the story of your suffering than you want to admit? Is God the cause of your pain? These are the questions of honest travel. These are the types of questions we have to answer for ourselves if we are ever going to see our anger at God dissipate like fog being burned off by the rising sun. We won't solve our suffering by doing this. It might not even lighten the burden. But we will begin to better see what our feet trip over. And our steps might become more sure as we walk toward the help we need to seek.

Chapter 6

Stories Told & Secondhand Truths

WE ARE EXHAUSTED AND frozen in a grieving process that leaves our hearts no room to wrestle with pain and God himself. We are acting and reacting to the world from a place of both anguish and trust. Both suffering and faith. Disbelief and belief. But where is our trust, faith, and belief anchored? The torment and binding of our pain have their own ways of instructing us, as we have already seen. The intrusion of death and decay in our lives weaves together a story of insinuation about the God of our faith. We are confronted by this story as it attempts to both unseat and twist beliefs we faithfully desire in the surrounding darkness of suffering and loss. But this is just one aspect of the truths informing us.

Speaking a truth does not amount to belief. We are handed truths that we accept without much reflection. As we will come to understand, these are "secondhand truths" we fail to make our own beliefs worth trusting. Our anger at God reveals what beliefs truly inform and feed us when confusion and pain take away our sight and ability to move freely. While we name and debunk lies we have come to believe, understanding secondhand truths will provide new traction as we attempt to find footing in our journey out of our anger at God. However, before we name these secondhand truths, we must confront the stories we have been told throughout lives marked by both pleasure and pain. We do not become God-angry believers in a vacuum. Instead, circumstances and relationships throughout our lives construct systems of beliefs, providing a spiritual and emotional home that allows us both to believe in and be angry with God.

Power of Belief

When faced with any number of different experiences, it seems that we have a set of words and actions preloaded into our fingers. All of us have a set of beliefs informing and fueling how we respond inside the relationships and events life throws our way. Beliefs root and nurture the thoughts, words, and actions flowing from our hearts and into the world.

We pick up beliefs in many different ways, and we don't always notice how and when we start trusting them. Before we think about where we get beliefs, we need to explore *what* beliefs are and *why* they matter inside our anger at God. We spend little time analyzing what informs our words and postures. The foggy confusion and exhaustion burden our shoulders and tie up our minds away from the difficult task of digging into our grieving hearts.

Beliefs are the currency of our actions and words. Beliefs are the stuff that makes up faith. We have trust in the certainty of what a belief tells us. A belief can be simple or complex, but it always follows a pattern. Beliefs are the statements that allow us to understand and process this life.

"God loves me, so he will give me good things." It's an easy enough statement, no matter the validity. It is a belief that, stated or unstated, leads to certain expectations and actions. But not all beliefs are so sanitary. "I am unlovable and unworthy of being loved." Before thinking about where such a belief comes from, notice the expectations and actions it requires of the believer. It will inform every relationship, even with God; further, it explains the pain the believer experiences. Some beliefs are outright brutal, while others feel warm and inviting. "God is a Father, so he will keep my children safe." Notice the expectations and actions involved. It's a hopeful belief, until sickness and death intrude on our children.

The expectations of these truths propel us into action because they have power. It might be too simple to say that we give them power, but it's true. There might be more at play, but not less. What we believe informs our actions. Our beliefs explain why we should act in certain ways. If I believe God has nothing but good things in store for me, I will expect and wait for the sun to greet me every day. I will be disoriented when rain pours or pain becomes a houseguest. We have been accumulating our beliefs in hopes of interpreting life. If beliefs are the truths and expectations we have about life and our relationships, where do they come from? And how did we come to gather them?

Stories Old and New

We are creatures living within stories. In all of us are narratives that give life meaning and orient how we inhabit our days. These are stories with characters resembling antiheroes and more gloom than we wish. Our lives are dramas unfolding at a pace we seldom approve. But it is within these very situated stories that we pick up our beliefs. Worse, sometimes it feels that more of the truths we believe about ourselves have been forced upon us. If we are going to penetrate what we truly believe (and how it has carried us into our anger at God), we need to see how easily we pick them up.

When we think about the power of the stories informing our inner lives, we need to understand just how old and strong most are. Without making endless references to therapeutic journals, it is clear that our parents are some of the strongest characters in our sagas. What our parents do or don't do, say or don't say, leave lasting impressions. They can last a lifetime. Such impressions are also left by parents who aren't even present. In so many ways these old stories and seminal characters provide much of the material we use as a guide to interpret other relationships and events we experience.

God designs parents to be influential and even painfully powerful in the lives of children. For better or worse, our parents give us many of the beliefs we use as a compass for our faith. The encouraging parent instills hope in a child, which helps her envision her own story; but an abandoned child loses that hope as he wonders why his parent left. Abusive parents also have shaping power. Children of alcoholics have a difficult time believing that there are safe places to be found outside the defenses they build for themselves. It wasn't until I experienced my own divorce that I began seeing how my parents' divorce shaped many of the beliefs I used to find equilibrium in life. With only my father's absence to guide me, long ago I tried to gain control over the unpredictable nature of my life by adopting the simple belief that he left because I was unlovable. With this simple interpretation, I found a way to make sense of the world around me. A life lived out of this belief didn't give me much hope in marriage. And as I stood watching my ex-wife drive out of my life, the word "again" dripped out of me with no hesitation. This is just one way our stories shape beliefs, even the beliefs that lead to our rage at God.

Some of us are suspicious that these old stories have any bearing on why we are angry at God. What do our parents or siblings, for example, have to do with what we believe about God? Perhaps nothing, or perhaps (almost) everything. If our parents are, in large part, the main shapers of our early formation, what do their performances have to say about the God who ordained us to be born (or adopted) into this specific family? Was your father indifferent toward you? Your mother too consumed with herself to truly see you? Was there abuse? Or was there more joy and peace than you can find words to explain? What does this say about God? Before we try to give a *biblically correct* response, try to give an answer actually coming from your bones. Try saying what you have been dying to express.

Now before we spend all of our energy trying to categorize the merit of these beliefs, we simply need to understand what beliefs we actually have. Do you see God as an extension of your father (for better or worse)? Was the ease or trials of your upbringing the beginning of what you expected your life to be? So much happens to us in childhood that we never truly move past it all, whether good or bad. These are the old stories we lived through and now try to interpret. They became some of the most fundamental and permeating beliefs we would live out.

Taking an honest look at what old stories helped us travel to certain beliefs is difficult but worthwhile. Somewhere we gathered a pile of beliefs, plucked from experiences, that collided with suffering, becoming more than we could handle. We felt left with no choice but to find God lacking.

In some ways we pick up these beliefs like bread crumbs, trying to find a way to make some sense out of life. But when these beliefs are poisonous to our souls, the sense we make is disorienting and backwards. They quickly become ingrained into the filter that sifts each life experiences. The older the story, the longer it gets relived. The more prominent the characters (parents, siblings, spouses, children), the more trustworthy the story is to us. The more tragic, the deeper the narrative digs itself into the heart.

While not all of us have tragic old stories, we all have narratives skewing the shade we use to color life. Some of the most surprising God-angry people I meet are ones with expectations of a *good life* because they grew up in a "Christian" home. Their parents were loving, hardly fought, and attended church. Inside these God-angry people, old stories watered a belief that if you loved God, do your best to live a "Christian" life, then good things should follow. But all these years later, after all the rules and Sunday worship gatherings, some devastating suffering rips apart the person's good life. A belief rooted in an old and "trusted" story becomes a foundational piece of what creates the God-angry believer.

Along with the old stories, we gained new narratives. In fact, we never stop gaining and cultivating our life stories. We can't. Even the numbest of people try to interpret all they experience. The son abandoned by his father becomes a father himself. Now what is he going to make of this new story in light of the old? Can he hold both chronicles at once? The abused daughter grows up and finds a man who wants to spend his life loving her. How does she make sense of this love being offered? Is it worth the risk based on the pain of her past story? Like old stories, new stories come with their own power to create, destroy, or cultivate the beliefs we

Part II: The Story of Our Anger at God

use to orient our faith. Just as we need to dig into our old stories, we also need to plunge into these newer ones. Is past pain informing new pain? Is present suffering smashing past beliefs of safety and security? Faith is put on display as we form our lives around beliefs we trust to give us the best chance at survival.

Before we classify our beliefs as right or wrong, we simply need to see them. It is not easy to spot our beliefs—especially when we don't always believe what we confess to believe. Oftentimes we see our beliefs come to the surface when we see the responses we have lived in old tales. We see the way we hid ourselves away from others because we came to believe there was no safe relationship to dwell inside. Or we see the way we came to believe God would protect our children from danger because that is what he seemed to do for us when we grew up in our Christian parents' home. Our experiences inside these stories become the most plausible and stable thing we can find to build our future hopes around, even if we come to believe brutal and shameful things about God and ourselves.

This is how our anger our anger at God began. We hold beliefs, grown in our life stories, which we assume give us a stable life we can somewhat control. We couldn't have seen it at the time, but small seeds of our anger at God were planted in the expectations of these beliefs. We thought he would act a certain way, but when he didn't, we felt that he failed to keep his end of the bargain. In our reactions, the suffering was the catalyst that exposed what we truly believe. We need to understand how these stories took us by the hand and guided us to certain beliefs. Not everyone who experiences the same events responds the same way. Our responses flow from beliefs cultivated before events of suffering and tragedy. What life events founded your beliefs? As hard as it is to swallow sometimes, we make choices about how we respond and how we believe. This means we are human. Not everything we believe turns out to be right or healthy. We do the best we can, especially when we are children attempting to navigate complex worlds with ramifications we cannot begin to understand at such a young age.

Looking back at old and newer stories is not a way to breed guilt or shame. This is not morbid investigation. We are only trying to find ways of clearing the fog of confusion. There is value in knowing "how we got here." But there is only devastation in using what we might find as a whip to beat ourselves. In the same light, it is also not an occasion to amplify our anger at God. But has anyone been able to stop us from being angry at him simply by telling us not to?

Secondhand Truths

We all do and say things that run contrary to what we say we believe. Because sin is a reality for all of us, we often sprint the opposite direction of our confessed faith. Does this mean that we do not truly believe what we claim? Should we begin to fear for our salvation? No. But we do need to understand *secondhand truths*.

As we saw when looking at how our stories create beliefs, we also need to consider that not all these beliefs are *functional beliefs*. Instead, some of what we pick up are only *confessed beliefs*. While the difference can be difficult to spot, they become clear when suffering thunders. A secondhand truth is a truth handed down to us from somewhere good and life-giving; but we disallow it to breathe such life into us and our relationship with God. They are beliefs about God which we confess to be true, but they don't actually inform how we live our lives. A good example of a secondhand truth is the idea of salvation being a free and undeserved gift that cannot be earned. Almost every believer believes something close to this idea of the word "grace." But where does such a belief go when we begin to work for God's acceptance as we attempt to be spouses, children, friends, and even pastors? In some way, we acknowledge the idea of grace to be true, but it is not the controlling belief that guides us.

Secondhand truths are agreeable doctrines, helpful counseling theories, and correct relational truths. They lead to peace and cultivate joy. But again, for some reason, we only mentally assent—store them away only as knowledge—to these truths as being needed for us to experience God and others in proper ways.[1]

---

1. Piper, *Help My Unbelief*, 48.

Part II: The Story of Our Anger at God

We all have these secondhand beliefs. We confess that God is good and trustworthy, yet we still question him and are suspicious that he won't come through on his promises. This causes us to take matters into our own hands. We believe he is good, but we do not live like he is in most areas of our lives. This is the essence of a secondhand truth.

None of us would say we doubt God is anything but truthful. We gladly affirm his holiness and perfection. But is what we confess what we functionally live out in our anger at him? Are we somehow *saying* and *doing* different things? Our anger comes from a very real place that questions and doubts God is who he says he is. When we attempt to only *think* about God, we are able to artificially *believe* many things that do not show up in our actual relationships. This is because these beliefs have not found a place of cultivation inside our hearts. We claim a belief without it informing the direction our hearts travel. "God is in control and has a good plan" is said on Sundays only to be trampled under the feet of our hard work and anxiety during the week. But how is it possible to somehow mentally assent to a truth when it fails to inform and grow our inner lives?

Earlier we talked about doubt, faith, and suffering growing at the same time (and often tangling themselves around each other). This is how secondhand truths stay with us. We see their merits, possibly even affirming their essential natures. We begin to use their language in conversations with other believers, pull them out to sound like good Christian folk. We have no problem naming their merits, but at the same time we have not begun to center ourselves around them. Instead, we continue to live like we learned such truths. We have what we confess to believe, and what we functionally believe. And it is out of these functional beliefs that we actually live our lives. Confessional beliefs might hang on our lips and even occasionally cause us to pause and reflect, but they have yet to actually guide our steps.

Naming secondhand truths is a part of the journey out of our anger at God. When we are able to see those things to which we only mentally assent, we begin to understand how we can claim

God is worthy of faith in one breath and then burn with fury in the next. We spot places where doubt still holds court in our inner lives. We might see the value of secondhand truths, but that doesn't mean we find them more precious than our own strength. When we wrestle with the difference between secondhand truths and actual faith, we see ourselves more clearly. We begin to see the places secondhand truths would be located if they had been planted and allowed to grow, taking up space in our inner lives. Secondhand truths have not been allowed to interact with how our hearts interpret life. This is the danger of secondhand truths staying in some mental sphere without affecting how we actually live. When these are truths about the character and worth of God, we find ourselves swimming in waters without the ability to float.

Explain how you can truly be a believer in Jesus, yet act out of emotions that question and rage against what he says about himself. I am not sure that both can be true without embracing this idea of secondhand truths. So where do secondhand truths live? If we hunt, where can we find them? We are not on a witch hunt. And we are not seeking prey to kill. Instead, we are trying to find places that are beautiful but not yet truly inhabited. We are searching for things that we want to keep, things that we need because they are morsels of peace and joy we are hungry to taste. The easiest place to find secondhand truths are where you smell the smoke of your anger at God.

Most of us are angry because we feel God did not do something we think he should have done. There is a question of his goodness attached to these anger pains. While we need to question if God actually said he would do what we think we wanted him to do, we also need to look at what allowed us to believe he would do such a thing in the first place. We will inevitably hear the word "but" where secondhand truths are located. "I know God is in control, *but* I am not sure he should let this happen." God being in control isn't allowed to interact with the situation because a question of his goodness is actually rooted in its place. It is subtle and all too familiar for us to notice. Even worse, secondhand truths can express reasons for guilt and shame: "I should know better," or, "I need to try harder." While secondhand truths contain beliefs worthy of our inner lives, when left unrooted they actually keep us from their subject and aim.

Lies That Starve and Feed

While there are plenty of truths that create our beliefs, there are also lies lurking in our hearts creating meaning and substance. It is not a stretch to say we have even been trying to feast upon these lies. But could some of the spiritual anemia we experience come from such a *banquet*?

The quickest way to find lies we believe is to track the shame we live with. But we don't just live *with* shame—we live *from* and *under* shame. Shame is nurtured by lies hiding in the shadows of our painful experiences. Lies create a narrative that sounds credible, one almost resembling truth. Lies produce enslavement, unlike truth which cultivates joy and freedom to move with creative grace. The difference is remarkable and heartbreaking.

One characteristic of a lie is how it twists and even embellishes truth. A lie might sound credible, even like an orthodox truth. But a lie leads to a shallow grave instead of a celebration of life. Lies also might sound safe and logical, but to the friends attempting to love us, the lie sounds obviously crazy and short-sighted. But friends are in danger when confronting our tightly held lies because (unlike a secondhand truth) we cling to them and fight on their behalf. Lies are entrenched in our hearts. We live from them and our beliefs are formed upon them, unlike secondhand truths.

The hardest lies to escape are ones learned from our old and painful stories. Lies give us a name we learn to conform to and offer a counterfeit freedom. But the name lies give reduces us into smaller versions of who we want to be. We hear ourselves named *weak, worthless, failure*, and many other banner lies fly over us. And the steady diet lies feed us lacks the spiritual nutrition our souls need. We might fill our mouths, but our souls are never full. Lies leave us dependent and weak.

The list of possible lies we are believing is endless, but the ends are the same: some level of shame and enslavement lived inside a narrative that moves us away from the sources designed to feed and enrich our soul. Unpacking our lies is not a quick or easy task. But that shouldn't keep us from the endeavor.

As we walk this part of our journey, we need new eyes to inspect this ground. Perhaps we have not noticed shame for what it is. We might even be holding hands that are perpetuating the lies enslaving us. The lies might be big and easy to spot. Or they might be small with large consequences that entrap us. But in all of this searching, we must not begin to feel a new shame for being foolish enough to believe them. We all have lies we believe. What are the lies you have been feeding on? Where is your shame found? Where do you go when you feel frightened or threatened? These are the places we find the lies we believe.

These lies are only a part of the larger reason for our rage. If we look at one facet at the expense of the others, we keep ourselves from experiencing the larger story we are designed to live. We must look for the lies as well as secondhand truths we have yet to actualize. We do this search inside the stack of old and new stories giving us the experiences we use to form beliefs. All of this is the fruit of our attempts to interpret our lives, the world, and God himself.

One More Thing about Abuse

Some of us have experienced abuses that are squarely at the center of our anger at God. And all of this talk about beliefs and lies might start to feel like a minimization. It's not. Being abused is not your fault. Someone choosing to perpetrate and prey on another person is awful. It creates pain that we should not have to experience. While we need to talk about the beliefs behind our own actions following our abuse, that conversation might need to wait.

For the abused, the best thing we can do is step into the grieving process and allow ourselves time. Lots of time. We need time to understand how our abuse is not our fault. Mourn the ways that our identities have been taken from us, even held hostage. The abused have nothing to be ashamed of, while the abuser should feel the weight of his despicable acts. Instead, the abused need to find our voices in talking about what has happened to us. None of this is easy or fast. It takes time and compassion, both from others and ourselves.

It is true that we are responsible for how we respond to being abused and mistreated. Many of us find it difficult to respond in ways other than shame, guilt, fear, and rage. While there will be time to explore our beliefs and subsequent actions, most of us first need to simply find courage to grieve. There is much to grieve over. More than we can even know from the places we currently stand. Fight the temptation to rush yourself out of some compulsion to *be better*. Don't let being a *good Christian* be an idea that keeps you from your grief. It's a lie. Grieving is what believers are called to do when they find injustice. Yes, we fight too, but sometimes we need to let others fight for us as we take an honest breath. The abused need to learn to breathe again.

Looking Out

So where are we in all of this? What are we to make of all the places we have walked in our talking about beliefs? How do we put all of this together? And what does all of this mean for our anger at God?

Our actions, words, and thoughts are driven by what we believe will give us the life we desire. Our hearts are filled with beliefs that are a mixed bag. Some beliefs are built on truths that are lifegiving; other beliefs are built on lies that rob and starve us. These beliefs produce shame and enslavement. Then there are truths we claim to believe, but they actually do not guide how we live. These are secondhand truths we mentally espouse yet never plant in the soil of our relationships with God and others. The tricky thing about such truths is the way we keep them within arm's reach. They appear to be rooted, but indeed they are not.

These beliefs, truth, and lies all come to us within stories we live and the characters that populate them. Our stories are raw information we use to interpret what we experience. Both painful and enjoyable stories are placed together as a filter to process what rattles around our hearts. We are trying to find some version of a good life we can feel safe and peaceful within. We are trying to find a way to construct beliefs that give us some measure of control over our lives.

Somewhere inside this soup of beliefs we create a picture of God and his performance. We find him lacking or untrustworthy with what is truly important to us. When suffering began to take away things we so desperately wanted, instead of stepping into grief, we opted for the anger that so easily rushed out of us. The anger kept us moving and churning instead of sitting in the stillness of grief: so we rush over our true pain and our true needs. Why? So we could come to a judgment that allows us to hold someone accountable for the suffering and evil we experience. Because God did not keep the bargains we thought we made with him, he was the best candidate for our rage and familiar distrust. This is the story of our pain and anger at God.

When we look at all of these pieces together, we see the detailed landscape we have hiked so far. It is a lot to see, catalog, and construct in our mind. We must take our time, yet always be mindful of the horizons still before us. It looks as beautiful as it does dangerous. We cannot keep ourselves from wanting to see it closer. But how do we make such a journey from the place in our story that only looks like a grand tragedy with us as the main character on center stage? We need a bigger story and a stronger lead character if we are ever going to find a way out of our anger at God.

Part III

The Story of an Abandoned God

Chapter 7

Where Is Jesus?

IT WASN'T THAT I didn't want to pray, because I did. I just wasn't convinced that it would make a difference. The sun was climbing in the morning sky, and I couldn't shake the pain telling me today was going to be just as agonizing as the last. It felt lonely. It wasn't a loneliness of absence, because I still believed in God's ability to be with me as I watched the sun rise on another day of depression. Instead, it was the loneliness I feel standing in a crowd. I could talk to God, but I wasn't sure he would understand. It's like a man trying to raise a daughter who gets parenting advice from a young single guy. It just doesn't help because the young guy hasn't experienced the weight of fatherhood. As the sun peeked out above the clouds, I whispered: "What could you possibly know about real pain?" God might be present, I thought, but he doesn't understand suffering because he doesn't suffer like this.

Jesus has more texts, conversations, songs, artwork, and theories surrounding him than any other person in history. He even divides history itself. Christians claim that he is somehow *the* answer to everything. In spite of all this, we God-angry believers have very little to say about Christ anymore.

I have never heard any of us say, "I am angry with Jesus." We have volumes to say about the God who angers us. We parrot platitudes about Jesus when wanting to avoid telling the truth about our anger, but we truly have nothing to say about the Son of God

PART III: THE STORY OF AN ABANDONED GOD

that moves our hearts. We have either become numb to him, or we have moved him to the margins of our lives in some way. Where did Jesus go? Or better yet, what god has taken his place?

In the first two parts of this book, we explored how the pain and wounds of suffering shrink our narratives and understandings about God and ourselves. We see how grief and exhaustion reveal what we functionally believe about God. We have begun to name our secondhand truths, which are our mental acknowledgments of God's character that nonetheless lack true belief in action. We also began locating lies that have silently led toward our anger.

We are seeing the ways we deal with grief and pain in our lives. As good church folk, we try to deny our questions and pain, all in the hope that they would just go away because we believed the lie that "time heals all wounds." Or we suffered under the lie telling us that "Christians don't question the eternal and sovereign God." But our denial only causes more pain and unanswered questions. As our pain piles up and our questions gain silent intensity, we begin demanding God answer for our suffering. Our anger steamrolls us into our fight against God. In some ways, this is our attempt to provoke God to answer our questions and acknowledge our sufferings. But like our attempts at denial, our indignation causes more pain. Now we need to see how all of this leads us to misplace and abandon the God we claim to know. If we are ever to journey out of our anger at God, we have to hear the story Jesus reveals about God. But even before we can truly hear his story, we need to take notice of the actual God we have targeted all along. This is our attempt to face the conflict between our suffering, our grief, and our God.

What God?

We know everything we think we should know about God. There is no more mystery to explore. We have questions, but not about beauty and praise. Instead, they are the issues of a courtroom cross-examination based on the evidence we use to build our case against God. He claims to be just, but experiences of suffering and evil show him to be the opposite in our eyes. Thousands of times we hear of his compassion and caring, but a heart exposed to the harsh winter of pain tells a different story. And all the lines about what a mighty God we serve? They blow hollowly over the desolate fields of losses forcefully received in spite of our prayers and pleading. We imagine we already know everything about him. We just can't decide (nor articulate) whether he is unjust, uncaring, or powerless. Or maybe he is all of these as he hides behind fancy theological words like "impassibility" and "sovereignty."

We get burned by pastors and friends throwing out God's supposed attributes and characteristics like Band-Aids for our gaping wounds. We need a systematic theology lesson as much as heroin addicts need clean needles. Because so much of our anger is tied up in suffering, we need something stronger than a list of God's characteristics plucked from a smattering of Bible verses. Instead, we need a story large enough to hold our sorrows and questions as it unfolds an epic greater than our own. We need to hear Jesus tell us God's story. But at this point, any "Jesus talk" will sound like more "attributes of God" Band-Aids until we get a clear picture of the God who has replaced our source of peace and healing.

In a sense, we will never see the God Jesus reveals as anything resembling worthy of our affection and trust until we come to terms with the ugliness of the God we have been raging against. This anger shows that we either believe God has lied to us, or he has abandoned us altogether. It is doubtful that our faith in him started with the image we have now. No one knowingly puts faith in a God who abandons his children out in the cold when they most need the shelter of compassion. Instead, our faith first burst forth because we hoped God could do something about the brokenness of our world and in us ourselves. Our hearts took a leap because we heard of a God who had a plan full of justice and grace for the hurting and confused. But if you listen to us talk about the God from whom we seek justice, this faithful God is gone.

Instead, you hear secondhand truths give birth to anger-churning beliefs: this God has no wing long enough to cover us from the blistering abuse of a harsh world. This God we talk about is no "present help." If he was ever close, he is distant now. If he ever had a plan, it failed. If he is the creator of this world, he truly has no clue what it is like to live in its decay. Because if he did, he would not let us be exposed to all this pain and misery. He would not let our good dreams wither as the rude and savage prosper. He must have left us to fend for ourselves because he could not (or would not) help.

The "god" of the God-angry believer is a formless and distant being who can only powerlessly shrug at the needs and questions of those suffering. Or he has the power to do something but doesn't care enough to use it. We are angry because here is a God who doesn't come through on the promises we believe he gave us. As victims of a cosmic scam artist, we want justice to be served. All of this is our best attempt to interpret God in light of our pain and isolation.

In the end, our anger at him shows that we have found God wanting and inadequate. Being angry with God is taking many steps past wrestling with him. We don't like how he decides to let things play out. At best, we are attempting to "freeze" God out of our lives as we sort through our pain on our own. We cannot get around how our anger speaks of a God who is inadequate at being faithful and just to those he claims to protect and cherish.

Who Is This God?

On Sundays, preachers don't wax eloquently about this false god our anger portrays. When we used to read our Bibles, this is not the God we found. Now we are beginning to see that we desire more than this false god who is deaf toward our blind rage. We are starting to ask the question, "Who is this God?" Because he is not the God we would create if we could do such a thing. And this certainly is not the God centuries of martyrs died proclaiming.

As we listen to ourselves describe the God we criticize, a sketch begins to form. We have been so consumed by our hurts and losses for so long that we have lost sight of the many words we vomit toward a God we think should be big enough to handle them. God has become a blur or smear on the canvas of our suffering. Our wounded hearts need us to take a moment and look at the God we create in our attempts to understand our pain. Our hearts have been roving and sojourning for peace amid this storm for far too long without finding peace. We continue to make this futile journey because there is still a vestige of hope in God being a place of healing. Our anger has taken away the one place where we hoped we could shelter ourselves during the blizzard—God himself. Jurgen Moltmann tells us, "Whatever can stand before the face of the crucified Christ is true Christian theology. What cannot stand there must disappear. This is especially true of what we say about God."[1]

In our anger toward him, God no longer has a name to us other than what we have called him all along: God. He is no longer Father; he is not a Son. And he certainly is not a comforting and empowering Spirit. He has become the same God of *goddamn*. He is nothing closer than a distant landlord refusing to fix a leaky water heater. Our anger flattens a triune God into a vague mush unable to be personal or loving. We didn't set out to unravel cosmic mysteries about the presence of evil in the world. We just want to know why God lets us suffer personally. Our pain is our focus. But as our questions go unanswered, our bitterness toward God picks up these cosmic implications like a snowball rolling down hill. And these personal questions can never untangle themselves from the larger context of the universe God claims to create. Even here we see the shrinking effect of pain. Even our concept of God is compacted, becoming only a caricature. We have blinded ourselves to the God we once found worthy of praise, all in the name of the tiny piece of property we inhabit amid the vast scope of history. We have robbed ourselves in our pursuit of justice.

In the end, we find ourselves standing over a God we feel we can judge. We just want answers from the God we know we can boldly approach with our pain and doubts. But somehow we find

---

1. Moltmann, *Crucified God*, x.

God as a vague, disinterested cosmic force with little desire (or power?) to do anything about the ragged and broken places in this world. "God help my unbelief" turns into, "God you are not worthy." We stand at a fork in the road: belief or disbelief. Or maybe we are the sick and dying standing in front of a hospital, wondering why we should walk through the door.

Is the God of our anger the God of the gospel? Is our angry sketch of God capable of proclaiming any kind of good news? Have we yelled enough at God to start listening to what he might have to say? Have we rested our case in the courtroom of our pain? At some point, God gets the chance to cross-examine the evidence we have presented against him. He even gets to call his own witness.

Do we have room for this God? Can we make the emotional and spiritual space to consider that we are poor artists when creating a portrait of God? It is this space we need to find if we are ever going to breathe air uncontaminated with our bitterness. There is a hunger for God that has been growing for a long time. In fact, it was our hunger for God that started us asking questions in the first place. And now that we have starved ourselves with this unsatisfying god, we might begin to cry out for the real God again.

Why Not Job?

Many wish to stop and look at Job as they try to deal with their suffering. They see an innocent man get something he doesn't deserve, which gives him the right to complain and boldly attempt to hold God accountable for the injustice he faces. Because we see Job this way (and even wish to see ourselves in this light), we find God disappointing us in his absent explanation of why Job suffered such great loss and pain. But I am not convinced Job had the right response to God.

We see Job pause and wait for God at the onset of his suffering. However, as the story unfolds, Job loses patience with God as the heavens remain silent. The more Job talks, the more he complains and grumbles. Because our own suffering and pain are so personal, we commend Job for such boldness and strong words against God.

Where Is Jesus?

We think we have found someone who can lead us through our suffering and help us force God to stand accountable for the injustices we face. We feel justified for the many words we have launched toward God because innocent Job is our shining example.

Job was honest with God, but I am not sure his venting is the proper response. The closer we look at Job's complaints, the more we see him slip out of rightfully lamenting his plight and fall into prideful grumbling against God. At some point, Job turns his words away from God and begins to complain about God. Tremper Longman notes:

> Job's words are more like the grumbling of the Israelites in the wilderness than like the laments in Psalms.... The Psalms are sufficient testimony that God welcomes our cries, but the book of Numbers attests to his disdain for complaints behind his back.[2]

In some ways, we look to Job because we see a man who looks like us. No one thinks he deserved the suffering and devastation that marked his life. No one wants to blame Job for not having the endurance and insight to go through his suffering in the right way. I'm not sure we ourselves know that right way to face pain and grief when we are in the throes of the initial onslaught. But we need remember Job as a flawed and sinful person, just like the rest of us. He did not get it right as he journeyed through the pain of loss and misery. It is true that he did not get things as wrong as his friends or even his wife. While Job is profoundly comforting as we wade into the murky waters of suffering, we need more than his example. In some ways, we have followed his example for far too long. Job is a comforting light, but all this time we have been begging for no one short of God himself to come close. We can all identify with Job's questions and struggles, but we want to know if God can identify with us.

I think most of us give Job too much credit because of the way the story begins and ends for us readers. As the story opens, we see the cosmic curtains pulled back and watch an unfathomable scene

---

2. Longman, *Job*, 106–7.

Part III: The Story of an Abandoned God

unfold. It's a scene that feels horribly wrong. God seems to make a wager with Satan, and Job's suffering begins. Then, as the book closes, God finally shows up to answer Job. But instead of addressing Job's questions, God angrily shows Job just how little he actually knows how the world works. Both scenes are astonishing and confusing. Why did God recommend Job for the suffering about to unfold? Why didn't God answer Job's questions? At the end of Job's story, we are left unsatisfied, scratching our heads.

Of course, Job speaks to us about suffering, but more than anything his story points to our need for wisdom. Wisdom is not the mental acknowledgment we know all too well. It is something far deeper. And if wisdom is what we need as we journey through our grief and suffering, Job doesn't have enough to offer. We need to look beyond Job because he is a mere shadow and sample of the wisdom we need. Wisdom is not a thing we gain; he is a person. We ultimately need the God-man Jesus, Wisdom himself, to help us understand God in the midst of our grief and anger. Few of us find our anger at God diminishing at the end of Job's story. His story is not big enough because God's heart toward us has not yet been revealed in Jesus. The questions still stand: Does God care? Can he identify with us in our suffering?

These are the unanswered questions that seemed to have lit the match of our anger as we suffered. But Job only hints and whispers of rumored answers to our questions. At the end of his book *The Question That Never Goes Away*, Philip Yancey sees these rumors in the amounts of what is restored to Job after his meeting with God. Yancey writes:

> God meticulously restored double all that he had lost: 14,000 sheep to replace 7,000; 6,000 camels to replace 3,000; 1,000 oxen and donkeys to replace 500. There is, however, one exception. Job lost seven sons and three daughters, and in the restoration he got seven sons and three daughters—the same number as before, not double.... Even this ancient story, written prior to revelation about heaven and eternal life, contains clues to a future resurrection. Job would someday receive double as he

rejoined his ten original children and introduced them to the ten who succeeded them.[3]

Room For This God

If we are ever going to complete the journey out of our anger at God, it will come by way of seeing and hearing from Jesus. We have been saying a lot of things about God in our anger, but Jesus doesn't seem to be informing much of our rage. We clearly mean what we yell at God, but does Jesus have much meaning to us lately? We might not like such a thought, but at some point we have to face the beliefs, emotions, and wounds informing our anger. If anger is a "secondary emotion" fueled by fears and hurts, we should not release ourselves from the implications. These fears and hurts have birthed a God whom we feel we can rightly judge, who has failed us. And somehow we have kept Jesus out of this version of God.

"Jesus is the visual aid which God has given to us, and which he wants us to use. To have seen Jesus is to have seen the Father," notes Alister McGrath.[4] We might feel that evoking Jesus is a cop-out or the crutch of a disappointing cliché in the face of our pain and confusion. But even still, can we begin to make room for Jesus possibly having something worth saying about our grief and suffering?

Somewhere on this journey we have to stop talking and listen. Faith in and a relationship with God is not a monologue. We have to allow our unanswered questions room for God to breathe. Of course, we are disenchanted with God because our questions have been left unanswered for so long already. But filling the air with our revolt against him has not gotten us any closer to what we desire. Could we have overlooked God as we felt crushed by our pain? Perhaps now, more than before, our anger can bear fruit as it reveals more about us than we knew before. Perhaps we can now hear Jesus speak to us of a God we never knew or pushed to the side. Will we let Jesus give us an account of his understanding of

3. Yancey, *Question That Never Goes Away*, 140.
4. McGrath, *What Was God Doing on the Cross?*, 40.

suffering? If it is justice we want from God, will we let Jesus speak about injustices he knows? These are not easy questions—but we cannot leave them unanswered.

We have to answer such questions before we can journey any further. As some friends and pastors have instructed us to do, we have been honest with God about how we feel about his performance. But I'm not sure we are experiencing any more freedom than we had before we got it off our chests. But up until this point, all we have done is unload our complaints with any language we want to use. Where has all of this unhindered honesty gotten us?

We like to say that "God is big enough" to take our honesty, and I believe that that is true as far as it goes. But I'm not sure that we have even extended God's enormity as far as we should. God is not only big enough to take our complaints and laments, but he is even bigger still! Somewhere along the journey from wrestling with God to our anger and judgment of him, we have forgotten against whom we shake our fists. By ignoring Jesus in our anger, we blind ourselves to God's own suffering, abandonment, and cries for justice.

We have spent the first half of this book digging into our stories; now we need to dig deeper into the story God has revealed about himself. We cannot do this without the Jesus we have been refusing to engage in our anger. Simply put, bitterness at God without considering Jesus is not being angry at God as he reveals himself. Our anger is the conclusion we made because we somehow felt the conflict has been between God and us. In our grief, we thought God was absent or somehow against us. But what would happen if we saw the conflict being between God and suffering itself? What would we see if we could make room in our brokenness to see God's pain? Would we see a picture of reconciliation? Again Moltmann shows us: "The more one understands the whole event of the cross as an event of God, the more any simple concept of God falls apart."[5]

Turning from our raging against God to face him feels like being crowded by a stranger in a room full of empty chairs. We all

---

5. Moltmann, *Crucified God*, 204.

enjoy friends sitting close no matter the number of empty seats. But we are suspicious and skeptical of a stranger who crowds us. We pull away when they come close. We feel estranged from God, especially Jesus. This estrangement is why we pushed Jesus to the margins in the first place. Now, it is hard to recognize him as he comes close. We wouldn't call him a stranger because good church folk know better than to say such things. We wouldn't call him unrecognizable because of the unhelpful mental assent of our secondhand truths we keep handy for such awkward moments. But our suspicion of him having something of value to give us reveals the estrangement. We have to make room for this familiar stranger. We need him to come close to tell us a story we have heard so many times before, but never enough.

Jesus knows what it is be abandoned and have his pleas go unanswered. If you are unmoved by the realization that you cannot be mad at God without being mad at Jesus, you should pause and consider why. Making room for others in our anger is one of the hardest things to do. But without doing so, any conversation or confrontation will only serve to inflame and fuel our anger. The same applies with our disappointment and bitterness with God. It's easier to stay angry than to release our demands for justice and retribution. We have to be willing to let God speak to the pain and anger as only he can. Are we ready to let him have space to move and talk to us again?

> Luke 24:13–35: Now that same day two of them were going to a village called Emmaus, about seven miles from Jerusalem. They were talking with each other about everything that had happened. As they talked and discussed these things with each other, Jesus himself came up and walked along with them; but they were kept from recognizing him. He asked them, "What are you discussing together as you walk along?" They stood still, their faces downcast. One of them, named Cleopas, asked him, "Are you only a visitor to Jerusalem and do not know the things that have happened there in these days?" "What things?" he asked. "About Jesus of Nazareth," they replied. "He was a prophet, powerful in word

Part III: The Story of an Abandoned God

and deed before God and all the people. The chief priests and our rulers handed him over to be sentenced to death, and they crucified him; but we had hoped that he was the one who was going to redeem Israel. And what is more, it is the third day since all this took place. In addition, some of our women amazed us. They went to the tomb early this morning but didn't find his body. They came and told us that they had seen a vision of angels, who said he was alive. Then some of our companions went to the tomb and found it just as the women had said, but him they did not see." He said to them, "How foolish you are, and how slow of heart to believe all that the prophets have spoken! Did not the Christ have to suffer these things and then enter his glory?" And beginning with Moses and all the Prophets, he explained to them what was said in all the Scriptures concerning himself. As they approached the village to which they were going, Jesus acted as if he were going farther. But they urged him strongly, "Stay with us, for it is nearly evening; the day is almost over." So he went in to stay with them. When he was at the table with them, he took bread, gave thanks, broke it and began to give it to them. Then their eyes were opened and they recognized him, and he disappeared from their sight. They asked each other, "Were not our hearts burning within us while he talked with us on the road and opened the Scriptures to us?" They got up and returned at once to Jerusalem. There they found the Eleven and those with them, assembled together and saying, "It is true! The Lord has risen and has appeared to Simon!" Then the two told what had happened on the way, and how Jesus was recognized by them when he broke the bread.

Chapter 8

God's Breaking

IF JESUS WERE TO take a walk with us and tell us just how much he understands our suffering and grief, where would he begin? Because we are still angry and bitter, we would probably expect him to start with the "tired" story of the cross. Even the thought of hearing a story about how he saved us tempts us to roll our eyes. But what if he started out our journey together with the words, "In the beginning"?

Luke 24 depicts a scene that helps us understand just how much room Jesus needs to tell us his story about God's own suffering. In verses 13–35, Luke recounts two of Jesus's followers walking and talking together when an unknown traveler joins them. The traveler asks them what they are discussing. Assuming the traveler to be out of touch with the latest news, the two men proceed to explain how Jesus died and apparently was raised back to life. It is at this point in their story the stranger tells these men more about their Messiah than they knew themselves. Verse 27 says, "And beginning with Moses and all the prophets, he interpreted to them in all the Scriptures the things concerning himself." They must have studied this man's face as much as they searched the words he spoke. Only at the end of the journey do the men finally recognize the stranger is Jesus himself.

PART III: THE STORY OF AN ABANDONED GOD

Like these men, we have become estranged from Jesus and do not recognize him when he comes close. Because anger does not just vanish, we have a hard time wanting to give Jesus room to speak to us. We question whether God's conflict is indeed with suffering and evil itself, instead of with us because of our anger at him. But even in this little bit of room we have made, Jesus can start telling us about a God who suffers great loss, experiences immense pain, and pleads for a love that doesn't get returned. Jesus starts in our cramped emotional space, expecting it to grow as our hearts slowly expand toward him. Jesus overcomes our estrangement by telling us of God as a heartbroken spouse, a sorrowful friend, a suffering Father, and the abandoned Son of God. In all of this, Jesus is unfolding a story large enough to hold our suffering and grief because it is a story about a God who himself suffers to defeat evil and death for the world he loves.

Understanding the Story

Jesus told lots of stories. But he wasn't telling these stories for the sake of being known as a good teacher and storyteller, nor to get wide acclaim. As N. T. Wright repeatedly points out, Jesus was telling these stories to reshape and explain the story of Israel, God's chosen people.[1] We have to understand how Israel's story is our story if we are going to see how Jesus has anything healing to say. This is not a theological exercise for the sake of another mental assent, like our secondhand truths. Instead, it is God himself telling us how and why he entered our time and history. It's like a husband telling his wife the story of their romance. Jesus is saying, "Let me tell you why I love you."

Jesus spent his ministry explaining how he is the One for whom the world had been longing. As he stood trial before the teachers and leaders of Israel—those who should have recognized him more than anyone else—he called himself "*I AM.*" This is the way God told Moses to identify who was sending him to rescue

---

1. Wright, *Jesus and the Victory of God*, 174.

God's chosen people from slavery in Egypt. In one small comment, Jesus is identifying himself as the God of creation itself, of Abraham, Isaac, and Jacob. Jesus labored to show himself to his people as the Word of God who spun the world into existence and who called to himself a people. If this is true, all of history hinges on Jesus being God himself who enters time and space to breath air and experience all that this broken world imposes on mankind. No matter how much emotional space we have been able to make so far, we are beginning to see that Jesus deserves far more. But the beautiful thing about this story is how Jesus expands small amounts of real estate until every inch of the cosmos, even our hearts, is called "new."

How does Jesus being God, something we already claim to believe, remotely touch our anger? What if God is accustomed to enduring hostility as he deals with the deeper matters of the heart? Even further, what if he is a God who takes the hostility of the world on himself so he can finally crush the true enemies—sin and death—of those whom he loves? While our hurts and fears keep us from traveling too far from our anger for fear of getting hurt again, God goes as far as it takes to get the healing and peace his people need. Even if he has to die in the process. If we can begin to see all of Jesus's talk about bringing the "kingdom of God" as his preparation to crush suffering and decay, we might start to see our anger lose its hold. The mental assent of our secondhand truths will sink to heart level, and lies will be shown to be what they truly are. We see how our sufferings and griefs have a greater context inside a story of God's own suffering and grief.

The story Jesus reshapes and explains is a long tale of God saving people who cannot save themselves, and renewing his creation. This story is littered with words like redemption, reconciliation, atonement, and many other terms that have become too familiar for us to feel their weight. Most of us spend the majority of our *saved* lives looking at Jesus in one way. This can possibly help us understand some of our reasons for the courtroom mentality of our anger at God. We seek justice to be served for our sufferings and griefs. We don't just pick up these ideas while we obsess over

TV criminal shows. We have grown accustomed to only seeing God's actions in this courtroom light. Most of us even choose to only look at the cross in such forensic terms. Jesus pays the price of our sins so we don't have to. The court finds him guilty on our behalf so we can hear the judge name us not guilty.

If this is the only way we choose to see Jesus, as right as it may be, we miss more of the story than we actually hear. As we already saw, there is actually something good swimming around in our anger at God. Corrupted as it is by our sin, our anger points to how, like God, we hate the brokenness of this world. This is also where our anger at God shows our lack of spiritual endurance to live in a decaying world without losing hope. We grow weary from the struggle, our vision begins to shallow, suffering smothers, grief becomes frozen in a broken cycle of failed attempts to bargain with God, and this one-dimensional Jesus gets easily pushed to the margins as we grow angry with God. Perhaps Jesus wouldn't be so easy to usher away if we experienced (again) the many images he uses to explain who God is and what happened on the cross he chose to bear.

Now, as we finally turn to Jesus's story about God, we need to remember a simple truth: God is about the rescuing, healing, and ultimate restoration of creation and people. In case we find ourselves getting lost in the details or running back to our one-dimensional Jesus, we need to plainly see now that Jesus is telling a story of God's unfolding and final victory over sin and death. This is the story of God choosing to taste the loneliness of a discarded spouse, feel the sorrow of broken friendship, suffer as a Father, and taste abandonment as a Son, all while he gains victory over what ails humanity and the cosmos alike. This is the true story of the God with whom we have been angry.

The Loneliness of a Spouse

> Mark 2:18–20: Now John's disciples and the Pharisees were fasting. And people came and said to him, "Why do John's disciples and the disciples of the Pharisees fast, but your disciples do not fast?" And Jesus said to them,

"Can the wedding guests fast while the bridegroom is with them? As long as they have the bridegroom with them, they cannot fast. The days will come when the bridegroom is taken away from them, and then they will fast in that day."

As Jesus answers questions about typical religious activities, he makes a plain reference to a well-known story in Israel's history. The last prophet to speak the word of the Lord before the fall of the northern kingdom of Israel was a man named Hosea. The kingdom of Israel has already split in two. Now, one of the kingdoms is on the verge of being ransacked and lost. Before the Assyrian army comes to cut down the kingdom, God sends Hosea to call out to the Israelites once more. God instructs Hosea to marry a woman he knows will betray the marriage covenant. Through Hosea's brutal marriage, God tells his people how they are likewise a whoring bride against him. Right before the Israelites experience the Assyrian siege, God pulls no punches as he explains his relationship with his chosen people in the hope that they would return to him:

> When the LORD first spoke through Hosea, the LORD said to Hosea, "Go, take to yourself a wife of whoredom and have children of whoredom, for the land commits great whoredom by forsaking the LORD." (1:2)

> For their mother has played the whore;
> she who conceived them has acted shamefully.
> For she said, "I will go after my lovers,
> who give me my bread and my water,
> my wool and my flax, my oil and my drink."
> (2:5)

> They shall eat, but not be satisfied;
> they shall play the whore, but not multiply,
> because they have forsaken the LORD
> to cherish whoredom, wine, and new wine,
> which take away the understanding.
> My people inquire of a piece of wood,

> and their walking staff gives them oracles.
> For a spirit of whoredom has led them astray,
> and they have left their God to play the whore.
>
> (4:10–12)

> For I desire steadfast love and not sacrifice,
> the knowledge of God rather than burnt offerings.
> But like Adam they transgressed the covenant;
> there they dealt faithlessly with me.
>
> (6:6–7)

When the ring slides on the finger and vows are proclaimed, a covenant is sealed with affection. Joy and hope boil between two people. Each says to the other, "I choose you!" No one else will do any more for the husband; he wants only her. A husband sets his eyes on his bride to be his desire and companion. He might walk out the door to go to work, but his heart is firmly entrenched in the embrace of the woman who welcomes him home when work is finished. There is hunger for her that drives him to make the covenant ring true every day. "I am yours and you are mine" is the tone and story. Chosen, set apart, desired, and loved. These all make up the economy of the covenant. The husband gives his wife his heart, the weapon that can hurt him most if she so chooses.

Rumors of unfaithfulness are hard enough. But betrayal is the weapon used to inflict oceans of pain. He returned as faithful as he left—but she left with no intention of returning. The house is empty and broken. He hears of her flaunting herself around town as he lies shattered and alone. The one he prizes now freely spreads herself to as many as she can. His heart crumbles as she breaks their covenant. As God's chosen people give themselves to idols, throwing themselves closer toward destruction and exile, this is how God explains their relationship with him.

God knows the loneliness and pain of suffering. He is a cuckold God who entered into a covenantal relationship with a bride he knew would break his heart repeatedly.[2] He chose to experience a

---

2. Goldingay, *Israel's Faith*, 344.

level of pain only capable by an unfaithful spouse. No matter how hard you try to numb or "just forget" the pain, the betrayal and abandonment stain the very fabric of the relationship. The death of a spouse has some sense of finality. But to be abandoned and betrayed by a lover who chooses another's arms is a wound repeated with every breath taken apart. It's a constant breaking.

As Jesus calls himself *the* Bridegroom, this is the broken marriage he describes. But there is an interesting reversal Jesus makes when he speaks of being the bridegroom. He says that there will be a day when he, the bridegroom, leaves. In Hosea, we see a picture of God not being able to leave or fully give up on his wayward bride. After saying that he will draw his people to himself and speak tenderly to them, in Hosea 2:19-20, God says, "And I will betroth you to me forever. I will betroth you to me in righteousness and in justice, in steadfast love and in mercy. I will betroth you to me in faithfulness. And you shall know the Lord." In Hosea, God's bride leaves to sacrifice her relationship with him for her own pleasure. When Jesus *the* bridegroom leaves, it will not be as a wayward spouse at the expense of his bride. Instead, Jesus leaves to die for her sake at his own expense. She will mourn the separation, but she will do so knowing the distance will reunite them forever.

As we simmer in our anger toward God, it's hard to come to terms with Jesus's description of God as a loving husband. This is not a God who is dispassionate and unaffected by us. This is not a God who distances himself from those he loves. Instead, this is a God whose beloved ripped herself away from his embrace. His arms are empty not because he crossed them to refuse his love. They are empty as she attempts to flee him. Most tend to have compassion for a person who is betrayed and abandoned by his or her spouse. We cannot help but feel for them. Should our anger toward God lessen as Jesus reveals the loneliness and pain God feels as a spouse with his whoring people?

Some of us are angry at God because he allowed us to experience the pain of an unfaithful or absent spouse. We cannot understand how he could let us go through such pain and still ask us to trust his good and caring nature. But Jesus refuses to let us think we go through our suffering alone. He also understands us well enough to know that we have a tendency to distrust and discount the advice of those who have not shared our similar experiences. Jesus seems to be showing us just how much further he has walked in our shoes than we have ourselves.

Because he chose to be in relationship with us, God knows loneliness and betrayal. Before the Apostle Paul ever picked up a pen to write about husbands needing to be like Jesus, Jesus was *the* husband to his bride. This is not a theological hoop Paul jumps through so he can whip sluggish men into shape. This is a palpable reality of God's love and care for his chosen people. He knows the pain that comes from giving yourself to another. The costs are high, even for God.

The Sorrow of a Friend

Everyone knows a true friend is hard to find. The importance of friendship to one's soul was not lost on Jesus or past generations of Israelites who wrote for the benefit of future generations. The book of Proverbs has much to say about identifying a true friend:

> A friend loves at all times. (17:17)

> A man of many companions may come to ruin.
> But there is a friend who sticks closer than a brother. (18:24)

> Better is open rebuke
> Than hidden love.
> Faithful are the wounds of a friend;
> Profuse are the kisses of an enemy. (27:5–6)

Anyone who reads these descriptions is probably flooded with painful thoughts: when a friend failed to be the comrade we needed; or when they used harsh words when talking about the most the vulnerable of places in our lives. Or perhaps we are stuck by the many times we ourselves failed and lost more friends than we gained.

God's Breaking

Many of us are angry with God because he allows us to feel the scorn of a cutting friendship. Nasty rumors and slanderous words spewed from the lips of our close confidants when it suited their needs and advancement. In so many ways friends can wound at a deep level, even having the ability to alter our personal and professional goals. Why would God allow them to do such things to us? Or why does he see fit to allow us to navigate so much of life without people willing to share such a relationship? Either way, we taste the bitterness of being scorned by a friend, and it is our hearts that take the brunt of the pain.

A friend can feel like a warm day of summer amid the harsh blizzard of winter. A friend can also blow the freezing cold when life shines warmth our way for a change. To have a true friend is to possess a jewel of untold worth. But even jewels can break glass when there is enough force behind them. Because friendships come in the shape of broken human beings, our most needed and trusted relationships have the chance to hurt us. So where does this leave us when we look at God, who allows these so-called friends to inflict so much pain and sorrow?

In John 15, Jesus makes some strong statements about friendship as he is on a collision course with the cross. Jesus surrounds himself with a small group of constant companions who never seem to understand his true identity, much less what he is trying to explain to them. But as Jesus comes ever closer to his painful death, he goes to great lengths to explain just how close he holds these men to his heart:

> This is my commandment, that you love one another as I have loved you. Greater love has no one than this, that someone lay down his life for his friends. You are my friends if you do what I command you. No longer do I call you servants, for the servant does not know what his master is doing; but I have called you friends, for all that I have heard from my Father I have made known to you. You did not choose me, but I chose you and appointed you that you should go and bear fruit and that your fruit should abide, so that whatever you ask the Father in my

PART III: THE STORY OF AN ABANDONED GOD

name, he may give it to you. These things I command you, so that you will love one another. (John 15:12–17)

What do you do when the God of the universe calls you friend instead of acquaintance, or even foe? How do you respond when God explains himself as a friend who is willing to die for your ultimate good? I am sure that these are words and questions the disciples wept over after Jesus's death. Jesus wasn't satisfied to call them servants; he had to name them friends. He couldn't let himself die on the cross without telling them how he had to have them in his life. As the disciples hid in darkness after Jesus's arrest and death, these words must have seared their hearts. Jesus never turned his back on them, but they all turned tail and ran when he needed them the most. They hid and denied Jesus to save their own skins as Jesus lost his flesh for them. "How could I call myself a friend?" they must have wondered as they thought of Jesus dying alone.

The God Jesus reveals is a God who is a true friend in a world full of broken vessels trying to hold water. Jesus experienced the sorrow of a friend's scorn when Judas sold him out; the hurt piled up when the rest of his friends ran and hid during his trial and beatings. On the cross, God became the ultimate picture of a scorned friend while he also shined as the only faithful friend found in all of creation. A friend is full of compassion and truth-telling. A friend forgives and moves even closer still. A friend pays when you don't have the ability. A friend will ultimately die if it secures your life. A friend does this even when he has been scorned and deserted. A friend can do this only when he has been transformed by the great commandment (love God, and love others as yourself). No one understood this better than Jesus as he hung on the cross to die, receiving the scorn of those he called friends.

The God Jesus shows us is made of stronger stuff than the weak God we have been trying to judge. It becomes a bit disorienting to yell, "Where were you when . . . ?" at a God who dies for the sake of others so they will understand just how much of a friend he truly is. Like a raging wave, our anger slams against Jesus's suffering, the levee that refuses to break. After hearing Jesus describe God this way, how can a believer stand in unmoved judgment?

This isn't a "Jesus is my homeboy" theology of pop culture. This is a theology with a full picture of the length to which God goes in pursuit of the urgent care his beloved friends need. When most of us angry believers hear sermons talk about Jesus doing something, we only hear, "Now go and do likewise!" Can there be anything more crushing and enraging? But, Jesus says, "I am the true friend for your sake! I do this because you cannot!"

The Suffering of a Father

In Luke 15, we find Jesus telling one of his most famous parables, "The Prodigal Son." Jesus speaks of a father who has two sons. While most of the story seems to focus on the younger son who demands his inheritance early and proceeds to squander all that is given, it is the elder son who seems to be left empty-handed as the story closes. But there is another person in the story who is constantly suffering. The father suffers the loss of both sons at different stages of the story. His house is never full from the moment the younger son leaves. Even when the younger son returns home, the older brother refuses to enter back into the home. Jesus, among many other things, is painting a picture of God as a Father who suffers at the hands of his children.

The younger son doesn't want the father; he only wants what the father will give him. "I don't want you," resounds in his asking for his share of the family estate. He takes the money and runs headlong into the life he thinks will bring him more fulfillment than being with his father and working in the fields for the good of the whole family. The son doesn't care what happens to the father, because now he has what he truly wanted all along.

This younger son leaves and spends his inheritance, becoming the life of the party, until he is facedown, contemplating eating with the most unclean of animals. He dreams of home and what it would be like to enter into his father's presence again. Would he be turned away? Would he be welcomed only if he becomes a servant to his father? What will he find when his father's eyes catch sight of him?

Part III: The Story of an Abandoned God

Because we know this story all too well, we have all but lost the awe and wonder of the father greeting his wandering son and restoring him. But have we missed something more in the familiarity? After the son leaves, we don't see the father again until the son begins to make his way up the driveway of the father's home. We see the father waiting on the porch. We get the impression that the father has been waiting for the son's return from the moment he left. Did the father get much sleep? What was it like for the father to carry the cultural shame of a wayward son? Because most of us focus on the journey of this prodigal son, the father's anguish and suffering are merely a backdrop of the story for us. But in our anger at God, we don't even think of this story.

Once the father sees his son, who is still far off, he picks up his robe and runs toward his boy. If the cultural shame his son gave him wasn't enough already, the father adds to it by showing his legs in public. He doesn't stop running until he reaches his son with a warm embrace. This father faces personal, familial, and cultural suffering for the sake of this child. He wants nothing to do with a son as a servant—he wants to party! He wants to use the resources he has left, after the son took and squandered his portion, to celebrate and rejoice. Every ounce of pain and anguish pales in comparison to the joy of having his son back. But even as the "welcome home" party was raging, the father's house is still not full.

The older brother, the one who dutifully stayed, comes to the house to get a closer look at the party. He has been told his younger brother has returned, and he is enraged by the party wasted on the one who lost an inheritance. The father leaves the celebration of a son being found to find yet another son who is refusing him. The eldest son publicly scolds his father for wasting what has now entirely become his inheritance. The father's love and presence was not enough for this son either. The story ends with the father outside waiting on a son. The party rages on, but the father cannot fully enjoy it because his house is still not yet full. The father has spared no expense, yet he still suffers loss. This is the God Jesus calls "Father."

God's Breaking

Once parents choose to raise a child, they choose to open themselves up to the assured pain and rejection the child will give them. Parents accept the suffering so they can love their children. This is how Jesus portrays God. God is a Father who willingly suffers indignity and pain for the sake of his children. In our anger, we believe God must not care or be affected by our plight and suffering. In the confusion and hurt, we cannot understand what God is doing, so we believe that he must not care as much as he claims. Or, like the eldest son, we neither like nor trust the way he does things, so we refuse the Father's pleading to come inside. Because we have spent so much time and energy trying not to be affected by God, but instead attempting to judge him, we are too exhausted to see how affected he is by us. In this way, we are both the younger and elder son rolled into one. We don't know what to do with a God who is willing to suffer like a father. But Jesus tells us God is like a Father who willingly enters into relationship with his children to suffer wounds only children can give—all for the sake of loving them until they return home forever.

God suffering as a father is seen most clearly when Jesus prays in the garden before he is arrested and when he cries out on the cross. We rightly focus on Jesus's pain and suffering as he bleeds during the garden prayer and on the cross. But what is happening to the Father as his Son was experiencing the suffering of sacrifice? If God chooses to enter into a relationship with us, chooses the pain he knows it will bring, how could we not see the suffering of the Father as his Son begs for the possibility of a different cup to drink? Then how could the divine Trinitarian relationship not hurt in some way as Jesus the man cries out and suffocates on the cross? Of course Jesus willingly chose the way of the cross for the sake of salvation, but it is a painful plan that included the Father being separated from his son as Jesus drank the cup of wrath. We can never provide a perfect formula to fully understand the mystery of how God accomplished all that he did through the cross. But it is safe to say that there wasn't an ounce of the Triune God not affected by the death of Jesus on the cross. Even in light of the eternal ramifications of reconciliation, God suffered. The God whom Jesus reveals to us is a God deeply affected by us. He hates the pain and sorrow we experience just as a parent hates to see his child suffer (even if there is a promised outcome of reconciliation). This is clearly not the picture of God we have painted in our anger and grief. In our grief, we have forgotten the suffering of God on our behalf.

Because his chosen children suffer, God chooses to suffer for their ultimate healing. We might not see it now, but neither our nor God's suffering is in vain. God suffered his children turning from him because he wanted them to be with him forever! God is a Father who is working toward an eternal victory over the true enemy of his children. Our grief has exhausted us, but God is not tired, nor is he taking a break from working things for the good of his children and his world. He is not searching for a Band-Aid to cover our wounds. He is a Father who will not settle for anything less than our total healing and peace.

The Abandonment of a Son

The numbers are staggering and always seem to be increasing: every day more and more children begin living their lives without their fathers in the picture. Divorce, teenage pregnancy, incarceration, death, or just plain abandonment can cause these horrible life situations. Some children know their fathers before they go away, and some don't. There are some children who live their lives as if they are perpetually standing at the door where their parents walked out, always waiting for them to come back. Some grow to hate both themselves and the absent parent. Blame gets placed on different people, but no matter where it lands, it doesn't stop the pain. No matter how old the child is, the abandonment is felt daily in one way or another; even if it goes unnamed and unacknowledged.

When my little girl was born, I felt the abandonment in a new way. On one hand, I felt the sheer joy of being the daddy to this beautiful little girl who could do nothing but cry, poop, and eat. In the first moments of her life, she had done nothing to earn my love, but she had it. On the other hand, I felt the pain of my father not being in my life. I wondered if he loved me when he first held me just as I did my little girl. As I tried to be brave and emotionally present for that little girl, I couldn't stop myself from feeling like an abandoned child myself. My hands were full as I held my little girl and prayed over her. But there was an emptiness in my soul that God made, only for a father to touch and mold.

Being left by a parent (for any reason, even death) is a torment from which most of us spend the rest of our lives trying to be free. Being abandoned feels like being unloved, even unlovable. Most children of divorce come to blame themselves for their parents' absence in one way or another. Other children who feel the abandonment of an angry or emotionally distant parent experience the same lonely agony. But all question if they could have done something to stop the abandonment. Those who face such pain have a hard time not igniting in anger against the God they know could have kept it from happening. To hear talk of God being a Father does little but reinforce our picture of him being as distant as the one who left us in the first place. All the sermons suggesting we should not hang our fathers' failures on our Heavenly Father feels like another call to "be better," to hurry up and get past old wounds.

No one knows what happened to Joseph after Jesus was born. Maybe he was around for a while, or maybe he died when Jesus was young. But most think Joseph died relatively early in Jesus's short life. What must it have been like for God-in-the-flesh to experience the loss of his earthly father? The Gospels are silent here, but I cannot stop thinking Jesus felt every bit of losing Joseph as we would. The father that once was there is gone. By the time we see Jesus weeping over the death of his friend Lazarus, he has already developed a righteous anger against death and its ability to rip people away from him. It is safe to say that when Jesus faced the cross, he was full of resentment and disdain for the abandonment death brings.

While the Gospels say little about Jesus's view of Joseph, they have much to say about how Jesus views God. He calls him Father. The Gospel writers give us two prayers where Jesus spoke most openly about how he (and all believers) has a divine Father in God. This Father has love, a plan, and an unwavering will for this world

PART III: THE STORY OF AN ABANDONED GOD

and his children. So what did it feel like for Jesus to face the cross as a son of this Father? What did it feel like for this father to stay silent as Jesus begged to drink from a different cup? What agony did he experience when the heavens revealed no other way for Jesus than a horrible death of being cursed on a tree? We don't have to guess what it felt like because Jesus screams it from the cross. It felt like being abandoned by the one person he needed the most. He was left alone to die between two strangers, surrounded by a bloodthirsty mob. As Moltmann says:

> He who proclaimed that the kingdom was near died abandoned by God. He who anticipated the future of God in miracles and in casting out demons died helpless on the cross. He who revealed the righteousness of God with an authority greater than Moses died according to the provisions of the law as a blasphemer. He who spread the love of God in his fellowship with the poor and the sinners met an ignoble end between two criminals on the cross.[3]

There has never been another person in existence to face the amount of pain and agony in such isolation. As Macleod says of Christ's agony:

> Golgotha was more awful than Jesus had envisaged in Gethsemane. He felt forsaken, and he was forsaken.... Beside the unanswered prayer there was the loss of filial consciousness. In the moment of dereliction, there is no sense of his own sonship.... In his self-image, he is no longer Son, but Sin.... No one was ever less prepared for such an experience than Jesus. As the eternal Word he had always been with God (John 1:1). As the incarnate Son the Father had always been with him (John 16:32). ... But now ... God was present only as displeased, expressing that displeasure with overwhelming force in all the circumstances of Calvary.[4]

Jesus was a son abandoned to feel the worst pain imaginable. The sky darkened as Jesus begged for comfort from his Father.

---

3. Moltmann, *Crucified God*, 125.
4. Macleod, *Person of Christ*, 176-77.

Even though Jesus willingly chose this path, it was more brutal than he could have imagined. After a life filled with the sustaining presence of God the Father, Jesus felt his father move away from him. For the Son of God, I imagine this was the greatest pain he experienced on the cross. The physical wounds were just insults to the injury of being abandoned. Just as we said earlier, there is no way the entire Trinity was not affected by the scene of Jesus's death on Golgotha's hill. Us trying to find a way to keep our anger is no excuse for us brushing aside this truth. God the Son died abandoned on a cross. No one had stronger questions about his Father's absence than Jesus himself. No one was abandoned more fully than Jesus on the cross. No one knows the sheer agony of losing a parent's presence more than Jesus Christ. Holding on to our anger at God is not worth missing this unbelievable truth.

When we only look at Jesus dying on the cross as the achievement of our personal forgiveness of sin, we miss so much of the picture. Jesus was abandoned so we could be found. Jesus was the greatest and most valuable ransom payment for the most valuable captives God sought to recover—us. On the cross, Jesus was enslaved to death so we could be set free. The guilty became innocent, of course; but God faced horrible suffering and rejection for the sake of those who would always find ways to distrust and compartmentalize him. Jesus suffered abandonment for the rescue of those discarded by others.

It can't be said any more clearly: God knows what it feels like to suffer the pain evil uses to drown us. Even if our anger is still strong after all of this, we cannot get around the fact that God knows our pain better than we do—and he hates it! God hates the pain his children feel, even if it leads to some better place. While the Father never needed a backup plan and he was pleased with the crushing sacrifice Jesus made, it grieves him that his children must travel through the painful thorns and thistles that death produce in this world. God himself hated the thistles as he walked on this earth. He died as an abandoned Son crowned with the thorns of this fractured existence we called life.

Part III: The Story of an Abandoned God

More Still

So many find strength and healing in "recovery ministries." These are ministries leveraging the best of traditional recovery groups such as Alcoholics and Narcotics Anonymous. So many in the church feel as if they are alone as they struggle, but few have the same to say of the support they find in these groups. When I first darkened the doors of a "recovery meeting," I found myself surrounded by others who understood what I was trying to express even though I didn't have the words. Sadly, for the first time I could remember, I didn't feel alone in the hurt. It was sad only because I had spent so many years following Christ without knowing how much he understood my hurt. We find comfort in and give trust to those who have walked in our shoes.

No recovery meeting or small chapter in a book like this can fully explain God. Not even the Bible can give us his fullness. It can be distressing to know that God designed this world in a way that gives us only enough knowledge of him to produce faith and worship. But it doesn't have to be so distressing if we remember how hard it is for us to explain our suffering to others. How can God explain all of his eternity to finite people so consumed with their own pain and grief? He knew that there would always be a longing to know more about him, especially when the pain becomes an unwelcome houseguest. So for reasons only God himself knows, we don't know enough to stand over him in the judgment of our anger. As believers, even angry ones, this is our good God, a God we can never get our arms around even as we long to be held by him. But our lack of knowledge of him doesn't hinder his knowledge of us and the pain of our plight. God might know more about the economy of relationships and this fallen world than we give him credit for.

God understands the utter loneliness this decaying world offers. Like those old-timers of recovery groups talking to the newcomers, God himself can say, "I've been there." But unlike those who populate recovery groups sharing their wisdom and hope, Wisdom—Jesus—himself shares his experience and hope with eternal understanding of how this whole story ends.

God's Breaking

God's story of suffering is about more than his ability to identify with our pain. But it is not less. We have to understand the closeness and deliberate understanding God has of suffering before we can walk much further in this journey. God has a resolution of the suffering and death we experience. But this resolution comes at his expense, not ours. Wright beautifully says:

> From within the story we already ought to perceive that this is going to be enormously costly for God himself. The loneliness of God looking for his partners Adam and Eve, in the garden; the grief of God before the flood; the head-shaking exasperation of God at Babel—all these, God knows, he will have to continue to experience. And worse—there will be numerous further acts of judgment as well as mercy as the story unfolds. But unfold it will. The overarching picture is of the sovereign Creator God who will continue to work within his world until blessing replaces curse, homecoming replaces exile, olive branches appear after the flood and a new family is created in which the scattered languages can be reunited.[5]

More than we understand, God suffers so he can be with us. There isn't a pain we experience that he doesn't know personally. He purposefully experienced the pain we feel. Our grief and suffering is bound up in our union with Jesus Christ. His suffering for our sake is his way of finishing the conflict with suffering and death.

Again, we have to pause and reflect on what we are feeling. Is our anger at God beginning to feel hollow as we survey God's own suffering on our behalf? Is our longing for his embrace starting to become painfully obvious? Are we beginning to see how sad it is that we have spent so much time punching the chest of the God who suffers just so he can be with us? Do God's sufferings and losses change the way we see ours? If not, hearing about how God will "one day" end our suffering forever will feel like more wishful thinking. God's suffering and grief have to be bigger than ours if we are ever going to find peace and joy because only he can actually do anything about what goes terribly wrong in this world.

---

5. Wright, *Evil and the Justice of God*, 53.

Chapter 9

God's Resolution

GOD IS NO STRANGER to the hurt and destruction death gives mankind. He is no stranger to the suffering and grief that man inflicts on one another in their relationships. Because God chooses to become a spouse to his people, a friend to the unfriendly, a father to the fatherless, and a son that drinks the entire cup of abandonment, he knows every relational space suffering and grief can wound. God comes close and shares the air we breathe. He could not let us face our suffering alone. He experiences every place pain and death haunts us. Where our pain is found, he invades. This is the God Jesus reveals to us. But there is more still to this story of our suffering God.

While it is always nice when someone enters the muck and mire to help, it does nothing to rid our world of the dirt and anguish. While we are thankful for the company, we long for someone to wipe away all the reason we needed help in the first place. It's a nice thought that God knows what it's like to walk in our shoes, but he still hasn't proven that he can do anything about the crumbling ground beneath our feet.

If we stop here, we are still left with a God who is powerless. All he can do is feel pain as we feel and die just like those loved one we have been grieving over. Is this as far as our relational God can go? Does he just feel our pain and walk this journey with us? Our anger has always been our attempt (no matter how badly an attempt it has been) to ask God if he can really do anything about what has gone so wrong with the world. We need the Triune God to be a divine spouse, friend, father, and son to know that he actually cares and wants to be in a relationship with us. But we also need God to be our divine warrior, perfect man, and victorious King with the power to put an end to death's crushing strength. We need God to feel our pain and make it stop forever. Can God truly and perfectly stand in our place, fight to protect us, and ultimately overcome what causes our suffering and grief? Our anger at him is enough proof that we have not settled this question. But as believers, we desperately cling to a shred of faith telling us that he is the One who can.

Jesus Is the Man

People hurt people. All of human history bears this out. Most of the pain we bitterly rolled into anger at God came directly from another person wounding us. Confused and hurt, we ask the heavens why God lets this happen to us. When the silence became more than we could bear, and God's people only piled on pithy statements, we raised our fists toward a God we thought was distant and unmoved by our experiences. But in this journey, we have come to see just how close he comes and how affected God is by our grief and sorrow. He knows the pain well. But what can he do about it? Most of those who share similar experiences can only walk with us through the devastation without any power to change why it happened or keep it from happening again. We now see that God willingly suffers because he loves us and therefore enters into relationship with us. So is he willing and able to come through with his promised power? Is he not only powerful, but good? Or is he just another suffering traveler who keeps us company as we try to journey through this frail and vicious world? Does Jesus, a man who can die at the hands of evil, have anything to offer us?

Every believer claims to know Jesus lived a life, died a death, and resurrected back to life to save us. For a moment, put aside the fact that most of us have little clue what all "saved" means, and just

Part III: The Story of an Abandoned God

look at Jesus. Jesus lived a perfect life. The perfection is not found in the way the world treated and received him. As we saw in the last chapter, Jesus experienced more pain, loss, grief, and sorrow than he could even image before actually being nailed to cross. Life isn't perfect here on earth, even for God. But somehow, amid the brutality of a world overrun with death, Jesus lived a perfect life of obedience and love. He loved God and people in such a way, all the time, that no one (not even the Father) could find fault in him. From the moment of its formation, all of creation has been waiting for a man to live a true-to-God human life. So can Jesus do anything about what has gone horribly wrong? Only if he can truly be human as God intended us to be. We can't just jump to the cross to answer this question. We have to go back to the beginning of everything to answer this question. We have to see Jesus as the *imago Dei*.

If we ever heard *imago Dei*, it was probably from a preacher trying to convince us that we all have a God-given dignity and worth. Then the preacher quickly goes into a rant about how Adam and Eve ate forbidden fruit and caused all of mankind to live as a type of broken mirror never able to rightly reflect God. Hopefully, somewhere in that sermon, the preacher pointed to Jesus dying so we broken mirrors can be put back together again. But how did Jesus become someone who could even die to secure such a restoration project? What does his own perfect life have to do with our fractures?

God called creation into existence with a shout of his Word. Jesus, the Word of God, was in creation from the beginning. God gathered the dust he created and breathed life into man. God gave man something he gave no other created thing: his own image, the *imago Dei*. This image is full of dignity and worth, a gift given to man. It is also a calling. God bestows on man a mantle of representing his glory to the rest of creation. Anywhere man goes, God calls him to reflect the beauty and glory he is created in. Like a representative dignitary, man is to represent God to all who come in contact with him. In essence, God gives man the keys to the kingdom.

God's Resolution

"Rule as I rule," God says. There is more worth and dignity here than we can imagine. But it is an image that always stands in a secondary position to the giver of the gift. To be truly human, an intact image bearer of God, is to live a life that points to God as greater than oneself and see creation (including other image bearers) flourish inside the reflective good of God. From the very beginning, loving God and loving others has always been the call on man's life. Man was to live forever as the *imago Dei*, being royal creators for the Creator.

But we all know this didn't happen. Adam and Eve didn't trust God when the Deceiver challenged their understanding and faith in him. They rebelled against God and all hell broke loose where peace and utter freedom once reigned. Being uncovered and vulnerable did not bring shame until humanity decided that they wanted more than God had given. Adam and Eve did not lose the image of God, but it was busted and smeared with the foulest of things: sin. Now every inch of creation would war against humanity, and man's own gift from God (the *imago Dei*) would feel like a carnival mirror always distorting reality. Since Genesis 3, we cannot live as we were intended. Instead of creating peace and harmony, we create sorrow and suffering. We were created to live forever, but now we die under the horrible pain of sin. There has not been a day since Genesis 3 the earth has not groaned for someone to live a truly human life as God intended. But all the prophets, priest, and kings fail. Death has its way with everyone, and sorrow never seems to end.

Then somewhere in the middle of a Bethlehem night, a baby cries after a very messy and painful birth. A star shines bright. Unnoticed by the world, God entered human history with skin on his bones, bearing the image of God. God becomes fully human. How will this play out? What will God do now that he is among us? What does this mean for that dusty idea of man being made in God's image? What will happen now that God has come as man bearing his own image? God does what the cosmos has been groaning for: he lives a life that fulfills and completes

Part III: The Story of an Abandoned God

the *imago Dei*. His perfect life is ripe with meaning for a world being crushed under a Genesis 3 reality. As Stanley Grenz notices, when Paul speaks of Jesus being the Last Adam, he is making a final commentary on Genesis.[1] In a world full of people who hurt people, God comes to love people just as he loves himself. In a world where people step on other people to get ahead, God comes to heal the wounded at his own expense. He wasn't just giving us a great example to live by—he was fulfilling the job of truly being the *imago Dei*. He did for us what we could not do for ourselves. He suffered like a sinful man, but not because he was sinful. He put God on display as he reflected God's glory perfectly. Where Adam failed, Jesus stood firm.

At the end of his perfect life, Jesus suffered *for* a suffering world. Jesus had to live a perfect life if there was to be room for all the sins of the world on the cross. Jesus took all the suffering of the world on himself, because that is what an image bearer of God does when he sees injustice and suffering. He does everything he can to stop sorrow and dehumanization everywhere he finds it. Jesus, the God-Man, the Image of God, saw grief and death everywhere so he did everything he could to bring about its end. The perfect man imaged God perfectly and did what God would do. He stood up for those who could not stand for themselves and died so he could put death in its grave. It's a fantastic story. So fantastic that it seems too good to be true. This is the "rub" for us God-angry believers: we are angry at a suffering God who perfectly lived a life for us because we could not live one ourselves. No one sacrifices himself for those who will constantly downplay and scoff at such love and compassion. But that is exactly what someone would do if he is living a life true to the image he bears.

When we looked at Jesus being the ultimate friend who doesn't let sorrow keep him from being a friend, we saw him fulfilling the *imago Dei*. As we watched Jesus be a lonely spouse to an unfaithful bride, we witness him reflecting the glory of God onto those who need it most. As Jesus sat under the pain of being an abandoned son, he painted for us an image of a God who never

---

1. Grenz, "Jesus as the Imago Dei," 617–28.

leaves. As he died, Jesus displayed a God who gives life at his own expense. And it is in his resurrection that Jesus fully completes the *imago Dei* which sinful humanity fractured.

If Jesus doesn't live after his death, he doesn't give humanity anything more than an amazing example to live by. If his resurrection doesn't happen, Jesus is just another dead man like Adam before him. If Jesus doesn't live forever, he does not restored the divine image God gifted to mankind. Death only came after sin entered the world. God always intended for man to live with him forever. The image of God is an eternal one. Death is the ultimate enemy of God's image. For Jesus to truly complete and restore the *imago Dei*, he has to overcome death and live in the eternal presence of the Father just as man was created to do.

When death stood laughing over Jesus's lifeless body, humanity's best chance seemed to be snubbed out. But when Jesus stood up, bearing the healing wounds of death's best attack, the beginning of death's end started. Man could now live forever because Jesus conquered death. Jesus's resurrection was the beginning of all things being made new, even humanity. Now Jesus became the first-born of a new people who, as God always intended, would live forever with bodies that death cannot break.[2]

Jesus, being *imago Dei*, takes away the ultimate power of death that caused man to suffer under its inevitable and final weight. God, not death, has the final power, in part because Jesus fulfilled and completed man's calling to bear out the image of God to the watching world. It becomes harder and harder to stay angry at God when we keep looking at Jesus.

God Is Our Warrior[3]

There hasn't been a "great" war for a long time. It has been at least a generation since the West has felt positively about a war it has entered. Most are conflicted about the enemies we are told to hate.

---

2. Ibid., 623.
3. Most of this section I owe to Tremper Longman and Daniel G. Reid and their vast study of the "divine warrior" motif in *God Is a Warrior*.

Part III: The Story of an Abandoned God

The word "evil" has been thrown around far too often to describe a country or people group. But the reality of terror is one all of us would like to see end. We might disagree with war, but there is no denying its reality in this broken world. There is a real Enemy that always lurks in the shadows pulling strings like an evil puppeteer. He is savage in his ways.

Being a pacifist or a gun rights advocate doesn't exclude any of us from a reality we refuse to acknowledge: there is a very real cosmic war that has been raging long before any country took up arms against another. Because it is mostly out of sight, it stays out of our minds. It is easy to forget when we sift our lives through a filter of seeing God as some kind of adversary against us and our good. This filter makes it almost impossible to think about God being a warrior who fights on our behalf against an enemy who hides behind things producing our sorrow. But if you have ever visited a hospital room or mourned at a funeral, you cannot keep your eyes closed to the horrors this enemy inflicts. It's enough to make you rage in anger. It can even lead us to scream at God, "Why won't you do something?" But as we are beginning to see, he is doing something and indeed has already done something about this roaming enemy. He fights against the enemies who war against him and his world. God is our divine warrior who fights on the front lines of battle and holds fast as our protective rear guard.

So what does it mean for us that God is a warrior? We have heard many theological descriptions about God that leave little impression on us. Is this idea of a warrior-God another way pastors and ivory tower theologians try to make us feel good about God amid our suffering? Or is this an incarnation of the "ultimate fighter" Jesus that became popular as pastors promoted their brand of manhood? Simply said: no. God being a warrior has nothing to do with men tapping into a type of masculinity or an academic pursuit. God fighting for and protecting the weak and oppressed are actions of a powerful and compassionate being. It is about God, yet again, doing for us what we cannot do for ourselves. It is another answer to our questions about God's ability and desire to heal and mend. If God is "mighty to save," it comes through warring against what holds us captive and inflicts sorrow.

The first time we most clearly see God showing up as warrior to fight on behalf of his people is during the Israelites' exodus from Egypt. God's chosen people are enslaved and being killed under the toil of a Pharaoh with no regard for any God other than himself. Over and over again, God does battle with the false gods of Egypt until Pharaoh tastes the death of his own bloodline. Every stronghold Egypt thought they had is defeated by God's fighting to secure the freedom of his people. God fights to end Israel's suffering at the hands of their enemies. In the end, like holding open a door, God moves a sea to the side so his people could walk to safety only to slam its waters victoriously on their enemy. This is *the* event Israel recalls when explaining their God. He is a God who fights and rescues.

God fights many more battles for Israel. But after hundreds of years of being exiled again, they began to wonder if God will ever fight for them again. Most of our stories echo such questions. It's neat that God fought in the past, but it doesn't look like he is battling these days. It seems that the nightly news always has mass shootings or acts of terror to remind us of evil's choke hold on this world. As we watch such horrible scenes play out in our neighborhoods and on our TVs, like Israel we long for evil's back to be broken.

When Jesus comes to the banks of the Jordan River where John was baptizing, he is not looking for a bath. Standing in the water with John, Jesus is being consecrated for battle as the armies of Israel had done. When he comes out of those waters, he goes directly to the front lines of the battle. He is led out to the desert to face the enemy directly. As Wright points out: "The biblical picture of the satan is thus of a nonhuman and nondivine quasi-personal force which seems bent on attacking and destroying creation in general and humankind in particular, and above all on thwarting God's project of remaking the world and human being in and through Jesus Christ and the Holy Spirit."[4] Jesus was tempted and

---

4. Wright, *Evil and the Justice of God*, 109.

Part III: The Story of an Abandoned God

challenged as Satan used powerful weapons against him. It was a forty-day battle that left Jesus physically depleted and spiritually needy for aid. Jesus then begins to take the fight to enemy. With every healing, mastery of natural forces, and exorcism, Jesus was pushing back the effects of death and decay. The enemy was not Rome or even the Pharisees in and of themselves. The enemy had been standing in the shadows behind those institutions. Now Jesus was taking aim at Satan and expelling his demons and reversing the destruction. When Jesus wept with violent anger at death's dealings with his friend, he was about to unleash his power. When Lazarus woke up from death, death itself was put on notice. The enemy's days are numbered because Jesus can overpower it at any moment. Now the enemy has no choice but make a play: kill this warrior-God on the battlefield.

Like a general willing to be captured in exchange for the freedom of his troops, Jesus chooses the way of the cross. Jesus dies on the cross fighting against Satan and death for the lives of the world. The warrior sacrifices himself for the greater good. When Christ took his last breath, Satan thought Jesus had died as his prisoner of war. Death gloated for three days as Jesus's tomb stood still. But when the stone rolled away, Jesus stood in victory. Death had done its worst, but it wasn't enough. The warrior had withstood the powerful onslaught of Satan. When Jesus walked out of his grave to live forever, the war was over. But like history records at the end of World War II, the defeated enemy still fought and killed as many as it could until the Allied forces finally closed out the war.

The suffering and death we experience now is the enemy being defiant until its bitter end. Like the parents and spouses who learned of their soldiers' deaths, we mourn what is broken by death and decay. We question why God still allows the enemy to roam among us without finally crushing his head. This is the greater reality of our anger at God. If he has already won the war against death by his own triumphal death and resurrection, why doesn't he finish suffering and death once and for all? Again we see how spiritually exhausted we are amid the greater reality of the cosmos.

God's Resolution

God understands how hard it is for us to fight for hope that seems forever delayed. How could we not be brought low under the enslaving weight of death's presence? This is why he fights for us. He is the warrior who fights our enemies and provided ultimate and eternal protection for us. When Jesus stood up from the grave, he was showing us what our future holds. Death does not have the power to end us, even if it still gets to bind us for a period of time.

It's hard to let the light of this truth break through the darkness of our suffering and grief. And God knows it will always be hard for us to understand. We cry out for answers but have a hard time listening to anything but the pain. As a God who suffers, he understands and comforts. And as a God who rages against those harming his world, he fights and defeats the intruder death. We don't like the idea of war because it causes so much suffering and loss. However, in God's chosen resolution to the conflict with suffering and death, he himself is the suffering warrior who dies to gain our victory. He takes the ultimate torment for our ultimate peace and healing. The conflict is indeed not against us (his beloved), but instead against the enemy who seeks to destroy and devour us. Jesus gets devoured so we can live.

However, his suffering is not for suffering's sake. Indeed, the ultimate goal of his suffering wasn't even so we could see how he understands our pain. The ultimate goal of his suffering and death was to put an end to death itself. Death and the curse is reversed through his suffering. This is God's resolution to our suffering. The war is over even if the enemy still refuses to lay down its weapons for now. The snake's head will be crushed once and for all. Death is laid in its own grave when all is said and done. God has the last word in this battle. But the fighting continues because he still has children lost behind enemy lines. The enemy will not release all of the captives yet. So God will not shout his last words until he has all of those he loves. Until then, we live with grief and pain as we experience suffering. But the story is not over yet. He doesn't expect us to fully understand because we are stuck inside the fog of war. We cannot see the entire battlefield clearly; we don't even see it as a battlefield sometimes. As the death count continues to rise, we cannot help but question. But we can begin to hope that God is not idle. He has not fallen back in retreat because the enemy is winning. Neither death nor suffering is the victor. The risen Christ is the victorious divine warrior who secures the ultimate victory for us.

The King's Victory

If Jesus is a warrior who conquers Satan and death through fighting, sacrificing himself, and then resurrecting, what does that mean for us and the entire cosmos? How is this a solution to all the sorrow and pain in the world? Warriors, or whole armies, fight on behalf of the people at the command of a leader. Most Americans feel that any leader who doesn't have the title of president is some lesser (or wrong) form of a government head. But God doesn't talk about himself as a president who upholds a cosmic democracy. Embedded in all of Jesus's talks about *the* kingdom being at hand is a clear message: "I am *the* true King." Through his resurrection, Jesus the divine warrior is rightfully seen as the King of the eminent kingdom of God. It is here, in the King's victory, where we place the final piece of our picture of God as he reveals himself. When answering the question of why Jesus came down from heaven, Aulen answers: "That he might destroy sin, overcome death, and give life to man."[5] This is something only a king can give to the people.

Countries and kingdoms can be full of good men. Armies can be populated by valiant warriors. But there can only be one king. God chooses to relate to us in paternal, marital, and familial ways so we can know how painfully close he comes to us needy and broken people. He understands our suffering because he chooses to walk the path of sorrow and pain. On that painful path Jesus becomes the man creation has always needed to perfectly love God and others. The path Jesus purposefully walks collides into the heart of the cosmic war being waged against God and his beloved creation. Jesus, the perfect man, is also the divine warrior fighting on behalf of those enslaved to death and sin. He dies rescuing the

---

5. Aulen, *Christus Victor*, 19.

God's Resolution

world, and then resurrects as the first fruits of the final victory of God. All victories are ascribed to the king of the victorious army. And Jesus is that King. In Jesus, we see a God far bigger than a churlish deity in our small, angry crosshairs.

It's hard to find a good king in history who truly puts the good of the kingdom ahead of himself. Peasants revolt against kings who oppress. But Jesus is a King willing to die for the sake of his people's freedom. He is a king who does not content himself to sit inside his lavish palace as his people face the harsh world on their own. He leaves the protection and comfort of his castle to be with his people. More than just leave the castle, he decided to bring the best of royal living to the people. This is what we see in the book of Revelation when the new heavens and new earth meet. As McGrath says well, "We do not have to climb some spiritual ladder to find God. He has come down to meet us where we are. And he doesn't leave us there. He takes us back up that ladder with him."[6] This is a different kind of king. This is the God-Man who is a Warrior-King.

When talking about Jesus being our warrior, death is described as an intruder. Death invaded God's creation through sin. God, being the protective warrior he is, cannot let the intruder stay in his creation. When we see Jesus as king, we see how there is no room in his kingdom for death. Death has laid waste and seized so much of creation when Jesus begins his earthly ministry and battle. When we look back over his life in light of his resurrection, we see how the King intrudes on death. As Bird notes:

> The exorcisms of Jesus are signs that the kingdom has "come upon you" as God invades demonic spaces and cleanses them by force (Matt 12:28 and Luke 11:20). What is present is . . . the kingly power of God over demonic forces.[7]

The King has no intention of losing his creation. Instead he wants to bring about its complete restoration. N. T. Wright further points out:

---

6. McGrath, *What Was God Doing*, 31.
7. Bird, *Evangelical Theology*, 249.

Part III: The Story of an Abandoned God

Evil is the force of anti-creation, anti-life, the force which opposes and seeks to deface and destroy God's good world of space, time and matter, and above all God's image-bearing human creatures. That is why death, as Paul saw so graphically in 1 Corinthians 15:26, is the final great enemy. But if in any sense this evil has been defeated—if it is true, as the Gospel writers have been trying to tell us, that evil at all levels and of all sorts had done its worst and that Jesus throughout his public career and supremely on the cross had dealt with it, taken its full force, exhausted it—why then, of course, death itself had no more power.[8]

But take one look around this world and it is clear that total restoration has not happened. Our reality is one of waiting for the promise to be fully fulfilled. The King has claimed his territory from the enemy, but the enemy is still fighting its losing battle. But even still, we have a King who stands in power and authority, even over the enemies who seem to control the world. Because of this, we need to see that Jesus being the King of all creation has everything to do with our sorrows and grief.

We, like the rest of creation, need Jesus on his throne. The crucifixion led people to believe that God was not there; however, the resurrection demonstrated his presence, purpose, and power at Calvary.[9] Jesus's resurrection as King makes his suffering the answer to the suffering of all the world. In the resurrected King Jesus, we see what the future will ultimately hold for us. Death will die, and suffering along with it. Even more, we will live forever with the King who purchased our freedom with his own royal life. Without Jesus enthroned, there is no end to the constant breaking of this world. To see Jesus as King is to acknowledge our need for him to be so. In our anger, we have been attempting to hold God accountable for our pain. If we are indeed "temples" of God himself, we have been burning against him in our rage. But as we look at Jesus as King, it becomes foolish to continue the self-inflicted holocaust.

8. Wright, *Evil and the Justice of God*, 89.
9. McGrath, *What Was God Doing*, 93.

God's Resolution

In our grief and exhaustion, we have lost our reverence for God. We have lost sight of how majestic God is. One rarely forgets the stature of a king when in his presence, but we have indeed forgotten. It is here where we come face to face with a king who is compassionate enough to suffer our insults because he loves us. It is here where we see our anger at God for what it is. It is petty at best, smacking of arrogance masquerading under our grief.

So, after nine chapters, we come to the defining question: is our anger at God sinful? At the beginning of this journey, we would have stiffened our necks and demanded the answer be "no." Our pain was all we could see when we looked at God. But now we are beginning to see how we cannot be angry at God without also being angry at Jesus. After all these pages, is there a way to justify such anger at such a sacrificing God? And now, with our eyes full of Jesus's royal image, is there any way to call our anger at God anything other than exhausted and painful folly? Or as Allender and Longman put it,

> It seems more accurate to say that our feelings are not any more or less sinful than our thoughts, desires, and behaviors. But God can use our emotions to disclose sin through revealing the depths of our battle with Him.[10]

Now What?

Most of us God-angry believers have forgotten the hope this beautiful image of God once gave us. When we first felt overcome by God, we longed for him to restore and heal us. We brought our brokenness to him because we believed he could mend what had been ripped apart. We always yearned for God to sit and mourn our losses with us. We hoped he could actually be what we needed him to be. We couldn't help but feel caught up in the inspiring heroics of him fighting for us. There was a place of allegiance in our hearts for our King. But as sin and death continued to pound away on our relationships and hopes, we grew tired of waiting. The grief

---

10. Allender and Longman, *Cry of the Soul*, ch. 2.

Part III: The Story of an Abandoned God

became more than we could bear. Our very real human proclivity to distrust and suppress God found new waters to swim in as our sorrows and suffering felt like an overpowering ocean. Faith in the "unseen but hoped for" collided with the world's powerful ability to harm. Our anger at God was kindled by our personal history and suffering. We became burning temples.

But what now? What do we do with this God who is full of compassion, suffering, and power? What do we do with a God who has chosen to bring an eventual end to our suffering and destroy the enemies—death and Satan—through his own suffering and death? God's resolution to our agony is to enter history and take upon himself all of the suffering death and Satan can give. God has chosen to restore his creation by being completely torn apart. But he has also chosen to wait to crush Satan and death for good. We live in a time when the King has come to announce and prove his powerful identity but still has business to do before he finally brings an end to death. What do we do now with our anger at this God?

We have to name our anger for what it is. We defined our anger at God as the premature quenching of our ability to grieve the sorrows of the heart. Our ability to grieve has been hijacked by sin. Because we lack the spiritual endurance to hope amid our sorrows, we did what all broken human beings in need of God's transformation do: we tried taking matters into our own hands. We made choices to find relief and comfort. It's hard to hope when devastated by sorrow and pain. God has always been an easy target because he made himself one for the sake of the world. So we took our aim at him. But now, we see a larger picture of him and ourselves. He is a holy God who is a Warrior-King who chooses to enter the fray of history to bring his restorative kingdom for the sake of the world he loves. And yet we are angry that he is taking so long to finish what he started. We have lost more than we ever wanted, and endured so much pain and suffering. We are exhausted and needy. And instead of falling into the arms of a God we believe to be our refuge, we pounded on his chest and cursed his name. Because of our pain, we dismissed the pain he willingly endures for our sake. Redemption and restoration are still unfolding as God planned. The good news for us is that this is not the end of the story. Because of all that Jesus has done, he can and will right all that has gone painfully wrong. If we let it, this news can bring hope even to us exhausted and angry believers. If we understand God in this way, we can understand our own history of suffering and the history of hope, in the history of God.[11]

Even now, some of us are not satisfied with the answers we find in God's resolution to the problem of evil and suffering. But even a lack of satisfaction does not have to keep us bound up in anger. As we saw in chapter 3, we unknowingly made some choices about how we would respond to our suffering. There is a moral action to our anger at God. We now have to make more choices. Will we plead with God to open our hearts to hope in him again? Will we choose to believe all that we have seen of him in the last three chapters, even if we do not like his timing? Will we move toward him in hope, or continue to wall ourselves off against his loving advances toward us?

Hope isn't going to happen all at once any more than a fire can be put out by a single drop of rain. It's a process, and a slow one at that. So we need to pause and take a breath. Let our hearts sit with the idea that the God whom Jesus reveals is far bigger and more powerful than the God patiently enduring our anger. Have we dealt with the fact that we cannot be angry at God without being angry at Jesus? If answering this question doesn't feel weighty, we need to ask ourselves why. Is Jesus still easily moved into the margins so you can take better aim at the God you want to accuse? There is a beauty and transformation God offers, even to us who are angry with him. Do we want transformation and healing, or do we still want to be angry at God? This is not an either/or relationship we have with God: it is a both/and. He loves us even though we are both angry at and hungry for him. But how we choose to be carried along by God in this story *is* up to us. We can either be surprised by the beauty and restoration he brings in spite of us, or we can grumble and be angry that the change doesn't come as

---

11. Moltmann, *Crucified God*, 256.

Part III: The Story of an Abandoned God

we desire. There comes a point where the exhaustion of our grief and sorrows can no longer be blamed for us digging our heels in against God. That time comes at a moment such as this, when we are face to face with the suffering, compassion, and power of Jesus. You cannot "make" yourself stop being angry at God. But you can begin to ask him to change your heart. Are you tired of being angry at a God you ultimately long to embrace? As N. T. Wright says,

> This isn't just a matter of "moving on" in the fashionable jargon. It's a matter of looking the past in the face, owning up to the grief which we often hide, and so laying a more solid foundation for what may be to come.... If God is at work he will do what he will do, and his purposes are always full of surprises. But I am convinced that when we bring our griefs and sorrows within the story of God's own grief and sorrow, and allow them to be held there, God is able to bring healing to us and new possibilities to our lives.[12]

---

12. Wright, *Christians at the Cross*, xv.

Part IV

Finding Our Story & Place

Chapter 10

Between Reality & the Quest for Satisfaction

It's not easy facing hard truths about ourselves. Most of us avoid them. But we can take some comfort in knowing we have done one of the most difficult things a person can do: be honest with ourselves while not turning away from how ugly such truths can be. So much of our pain and beliefs have gnarled root causes hidden from us.

As difficult as it has been to look at ugly lies and secondhand truths, even facing God has been an epic struggle. It is hard to give someone with whom we are angry space to stand in front of us without cutting their legs out from under them. It's hard to trust a person you think has hurt you, and it's hard to listen to a person you are angry with. But somehow we have begun to give both ourselves and God space to move toward one another. We even might begin to feel our hearts being moved in ways we thought we would never feel again.

St. Augustine is famous for saying, "Grant, Lord, that I may know myself that I may know thee." In fact, you can't have a clear picture of one without the other. All of our journey has been regaining our sight. But as our eyes began to focus on Jesus, we also started to taste. There has been a hunger in us unsatisfied by anything short of God. But we are starting to again be nourished by his presence and love for us. Where we once felt abandoned, we see his presence. But in all of our journeying toward God, we still have questions that haven't been answered. There is still a hesitation in fully giving ourselves over to a God who doesn't explain things that are so personal to us. As we stand on the banks of anger and trust, what do we do with this unsatisfying feeling? Now that we see God's story as the greater context for our story, how do we find our place with him? After we have seen what horrors we have seen, said the things we have said in anger, and invested so much of ourselves to fighting for justice against God, what does it look like to have faith with so much still left undone?

Unanswered Questions

It is unsatisfying to a child when a parent answers their question with "because I said so." You can see the child lose whatever mind she has at this response (then you can see the parent lose his mind when the child continues to ask "why"). We should not feel belittled when we are told how much we resemble children. Children ask questions with answers they cannot fully understand. This doesn't have to anger us if we can see how unanswered questions fit into the faith we need to move toward freedom.

If we wait to make a decision until we have all of our questions answered, most decisions would not be made. Faith requires stepping into unknown places in the hope of finding something worthwhile. It is believing without having all the answers to all of our questions. This is not a blind trust nor an unintelligent wager. Some might argue such a request is asking us to leave our intellect at the door. But that is the furthest thing from what God defines as faith, even for those already believing. What does it mean for us to walk toward God with a faith that includes unanswered questions?

Honestly, it means a life with many opportunities to doubt and rekindle our anger at God. God is not going to answer all of our questions. Not right now. And when we ask for a reason why, the simple truth is we won't understand. It is not a matter of intellect or maturity. It's a matter of infinite and finite. There is no way for us to understand everything we desire to know. There are

Between Reality & the Quest for Satisfaction

reasons we can find for "why" evil and suffering are allowed by God to exist in the world. There are even reasons why our personal suffering exists. But don't we get mad when televangelists spout these reasons after tragedies? Don't they seem to belittle and rob those who are suffering? Is there some truth to the answers to our big questions? I guess. But are those answers ever big enough to include the entire story of God's love and care amid his specific plan for you and the entire world? Probably not. How can our finite minds fully grasp all an infinite being does? It cannot. We cannot. And this means many of our questions feel like they go unanswered.

Those of us suffering need compassion and relational presence more than answers. We need room to sit in silence as well as room to be held. We need hope that there is more to the situation than we can see and understand. And if we have learned anything about Jesus in all of this, it is how compassionate and present he is. It is no small thing that when God suffered under the weight of the world's sorrow, he cried out "why." Jesus himself couldn't keep from asking questions that would not be answered before his death. Asking our questions is not wrong nor a lack of faith. However, demanding answers as a prerequisite to our trust and obedience is. Jesus asked his questions as he faithfully walked the path of suffering and crucifixion. If Jesus didn't have all of his questions answered, why do we think we should?

We have to accept unanswered questions and mystery as a fact of life in this broken world. But, even if God did answer all of our questions about suffering and loss, it wouldn't change much of anything. Getting answers doesn't bring back those we have lost, and doesn't keep us from experiencing pain. We like to think that if we had more knowledge about the situation we would somehow hurt less. But it just isn't true. Much of what we are really asking for in our questions is if God can find another way for us go through life other than a path of suffering and hurt. Answers don't change this fallen world. And knowledge has a way of puffing us up instead of bringing us the rest we need.

Your anger at God, even if that God is Jesus, won't be extinguished because he gives you a personal interview and answers all of your questions. In fact, we tend to use knowledge as the currency of our self-sufficiency. We think that our ability to understand all of this life will somehow allow us to live it better. But what if the way to live amid the brokenness of our sorrow has nothing to do with our ability and everything to do with God's? What if God's ability to understand and answer all of our "why" questions is more important than him handing us an explanation? What if Jesus's ability to live amid the mystery and unknown is more important than us having every intellectual and emotional problem solved? It's not bad that we don't have all the answers. It's not even bad that God seems to refuse to give them to us. What would be a bad thing is if God didn't have the answers and ability. If God didn't have the answers to the questions over the presence of evil in this world, it would be foolish for us to put our faith in him. His right to keep those answers from us at this point is not grounds for our anger or refusal to walk toward him in faith. Getting our questions answered is not the goal of a believer's life, and it is not the key to ending our anger at God. Instead, mystery and tension are realities of faith. Unanswered questions are as much a part of our story as God's grace.

Unsatisfying Answers

Even as we come to terms with unanswered questions, there are still unsatisfying answers looming in the ether. On our journey, there are answers we find that leave us uneasy and unsatisfied. Most of the believers I respect have a list of God's answers they would answer differently if they were in his shoes. Get someone to let their guard down (even seminary professors and pastors) and you will find even the most devout of Christians does not like everything God does. But what if being satisfied or having enough faith to trust in God wasn't based on liking all of the answers we find during our search for who he is and what he is doing?

Between Reality & the Quest for Satisfaction

All relationships have moments that leave us unsatisfied by someone. As much as I love and cherish my wife, some of her reasons for doing things are not what I would call "good enough." When we feel wronged by someone, there is a good chance we will not like the reason for her actions. But does that end the relationship? There is not a relationship we have (even with God) that will fully satisfy us this side of Revelation 21 becoming reality. We might sing songs about being fully satisfied with Jesus, but at best we sing them in the hope it will be true one day. So even after our sketch of God in the last section, we can still want more from God than what we feel he has given us.

I know plenty of Reformed believers who have a hard time being satisfied with all five points of Calvinism. I also know plenty of Armenian believers who are not totally satisfied with all the answers they have about God and our works. The reason doesn't have to be a simple right/wrong theological framework of redemption. Instead, none of us knows how to be fully satisfied with God and his ways because we are not God. More than just not being God, we are sinful, blind, and hungry. All of us. Somewhere in our deepest beings, we have to find peace with the fact that we will always want more from God than we feel he gives us on this side of suffering and death being wiped away for good. It is hard for a person bent by sin to fully love all of God's ways. Being fully satisfied with God is not the definition of faith nor the key that unlocks us from this anger toward him.

Liking and trusting are not the same things. And God isn't trying to force us to like all of the answers we get about why suffering and pain are a part of this world. In fact, there is a place for discontentment in our faith. Truthfully, we are too content with the way things are. Some of our anger at God is rooted in how he allowed suffering and pain to disrupt the little piece of heaven we have been trying carve out for ourselves. When God allows pain to disrupt and crowd us, we are unsatisfied. Or more to the point, we are not okay with his timing. We like the sound of him making all things new and wiping away all sorrow. But hate how long it is taking him to see the plan through. We plead for him to come "now," but he seemed to say "not yet." And that is not good enough. Why does he allow children to die horrible deaths? Any answer we hear will not quench the sadness of that reality. These questions can roll on for miles. But is there a way to trust his goodness and plan even if we wish he would make another way?

Jesus asked for another way when he was sweaty and bleeding in the garden even before the beating began. He pleaded for a different answer than the one he felt the Father gave. Some of us might be tempted to roll our eyes at another rehearsal of this famous scene, but don't give in to the bitterness and cynicism we have simmered in all this time. Look at God pleading for a different answer than the one heaven gave. Look at Jesus being unsettled by the way God's plan was about to unfold. Even our best attempts to theologize away this mystery do not ease the tension. But then look at Jesus walking in faith, even as he wished for a different path to travel. Not being satisfied with God's answers did not keep Jesus from the cross. And it should not keep us from looking to his cross either.

Unequaled Motives

It's not hard to see the war going on inside us. In the face of God, we recognize both our desire for him and our longing to stand alone. Within the inner life of all of us is a tension between unequalled motives. We are motivated to seek God in our need just as we are motivated to find a weapon to defend ourselves against him when our desire for the good life is being threatened. We want to be at peace with him, but feel the need to hold both a shield and sword to oppose him. We want to trust in the God Jesus reveals to us, but can never fully shake the images of God being just in allowing us to suffer.

We will always be a mixed bag of hope and despair, joy and sorrow, peace and war, laughter and weeping, belief and unbelief. The questions that feel presently unanswered give us an opportunity to return to our anger and judgment against God. And the unsatisfying answers we receive do little more to silence our demands for future peace to become a present reality. What are we

Between Reality & the Quest for Satisfaction

to do with our personal history of suffering and anger on the one hand, and God's own larger story of redemption through his own sorrow? Is there a secret to discover that will allow us to seamlessly sew these stories together? Are we even called to be such tailors and seamstresses?

I am not sure we are supposed to endeavor in such a quilting project. Instead, the idea of journeying has an honest sound when we talk about the inner life of our hearts. When we walk toward a larger horizon we begin to see how our story is already nestled into a larger reality than we once noticed. Our little pieces of real estate are only a fraction of the greater landscape. This does not mean our story is insignificant. Instead it means our story cannot be understood if we attempt to make it the entire story. We have seen this in the way we made our journey so far. The mountains are connected to the valleys, just as the tree is halfway buried in the earth with its giant root system stretching into the depths of the soil.

Our mixed intentions and desires are proof that our personal story is not big enough to hold the entire story of this world. Seeing God's greater story keeps us from "living and dying" with every fluctuating desire and intention we feel. The reality of our life is not reformed by a victory in our search of answers for the deeper questions embedded inside our anger at God. This life is not designed to answer all the questions. As infuriating as that can be to the hurting and confused, it can also be a gift. But does this mean that we stop all of our pursuit to make sense of the story? No, but it does call us to reconsider much of what we think we know about how to pursue.

If we are a mixture of healing and hurtful insights and motives, we need to find an honest way of seeking truth and peace. We need to find ways to both admit and change our faulty notions about God, ourselves, and the world. We want what we want. And for the longest time, that has simply been to be angry at God for allowing our pain to come to us. But we have also desired to see the truth of God's suffering and love. This makes most of our pursuit feel like running in circles. We need to admit that our contradicting inner lives keeps us from seeing a larger story that is being unfolded around us. We stand still more than try to venture out. We want things fixed and our comfort restored more than we desire to pursue a wild story of redemption and reconciliation. We want to be satisfied more than we want to be left in awe of the grandeur of the vast unknown. We want proof of our soon-arriving relief more than we want to live with the burdens of faith.

But, if we have begun taking an honest look at our story, begun to grieve and rest, and also started opening ourselves up to make room for God, then we can begin to find faith a more inviting place to stand. Trying to live out of a greater story than our own crafted narrative takes more than finding satisfying answers and stronger emotional muscles. It indeed takes a faith that does not dismiss God's story or our own. Instead, it becomes a journey into both stories with a hope in something outside of our ability to make sense of suffering. Is such a faith possible?

Understanding Faith

Faith is at the center of our ability to live inside a story that is wholly ours, but paradoxically not about us. Faith might be the only way we can continue to journey out of our anger at God. We have already seen the beliefs we have been putting our faith in, and how our anger at God is the consequence of putting our faith inside such a small narrative. So what is the type of faith we need if we are to continue our journey inside a larger story that feels so unpredictable and unfinished?

We need a faith that has room for both our story and God's own suffering. This is not an easy faith to find (if the word *find* is even the right way of speaking of it). Most of what we have seen in our searching is how much of our life has been spent doing violence to one or the other. We want to banish one or the other in an attempt to relieve some of the tension we feel or to remove the unnerving paradox we cannot get our arms around. But we need a faith that calls both our suffering and God's own suffering true.

We tend to think about faith as finding a truth that produces or validates some explanation we have for how the universe works.

Between Reality & the Quest for Satisfaction

Most of us get so caught up in trying to prove our own existential worth that we forget the truth of others' existences—even God's. But faith is not proving God's existence or ours. It's not even a process of validation. Faith might be our answers to the big questions of life, but it involves small movements of increasing our ability to both see and taste who we are and who God is.

After all our journeying through our story and grief, we notice how we have put too much or too little importance in the histories we have been formed by. We also see the power we have given others to direct and shape what we believe and how we live from such beliefs. Good and bad, the truth of our story must have room to reside inside the beliefs we live from. If we cannot allow ourselves to be found in our faith, then we begin to, as we have done before, do violence to ourselves. We exclude and crush who we are in an attempt to make ourselves into some version of who we think we need to be. Finding ourselves inside our faith is not having faith in ourselves. We are not attempting to become the objects of our hopes. Instead, we are allowing the truth about us (no matter how ugly) to stand in the presence of what we believe is true about the world and the God who created it. We don't exclude ourselves either as an exception or as some failed falsehood of humanity. Our faith must have grace and room for our whole selves; otherwise, our faith will leave us out in the cold of an ever-increasing hell that cannot let redemption reach us.

In the same way, our faith must have room for the God whom Jesus reveals to us. Our ideas about who God is and what he does must include his suffering as much as it includes his glory and ultimate victory over death and decay. For far too long we have allowed our vision of God to exclude Jesus because of the pain we have experienced. Our anger has been our violent and forceful attempt to demand God be who we say he is. But the faith we need, if we are to journey out of this anger, must instead have room for God to be who he is instead of who are demanding him to be. This faith has to allow God's own suffering to be as true as our own. Such a faith has to see God's plan and ability to see it through as being as important as the longing we have to see our suffering end.

Part IV: Finding Our Story & Place

If we are ever to have a faith that sustains the harsh truth of the present fallen world, it must include a hope in the reality of God that we cannot fully know and understand.

Such a faith will be filled with suffering as much as it is filled with joy. It will include unsatisfying answers as much as we find hope in other answers we come to understand. As hard as it will be to handle, such a faith will see so many important questions lay unanswered until this fallen world is finally renewed. Nevertheless, this faith will have the ability to welcome us as much as it welcomes God. We will not have to deny or hide our existence in this faith because God does not ask us to do either. Instead, we can be wholly present, bringing all of the life we have lived, without fear of being turned away or dismissed. Our redemption is as true as our suffering inside this faith. The greater story of God is welcomed also. Here God suffers as much as he rules in power. He is holy and compassionate. He is a suffering servant and a mighty warrior. He died and vanquished our enemies. He longs for our total healing and redemption and he also waits to bring it about. Such a faith can sustain us as we journey toward freedom and joy because we find ourselves accepted instead of an embarrassment. This faith can sustain because it is not based on our ability to overcome our suffering or even to make sense of its existence. Instead we are free to feel and grieve while God does what only he is able to do. This faith does not shortchange us or God. Instead our entire presence is welcomed in his own. His hurt and suffering begins to inform our suffering. His resolution to death's intrusion slowly is welcomed by us. His crucifixion becomes our healing. His abandonment on our behalf becomes our welcome home invitation. His ability to fight for us becomes our reasons to put down our weapons and rest. This is the faith that will allow us to place ourselves inside the protection of God instead of raging against him. We begin to see our story inside—not against or beside—God's story. Our secondhand truths begin to take root in this story. This is the faith that allows us honest travel as we live in a time of waiting and hoping. In a time of now and not yet.

Chapter 11

Between Now & Then

I WAS DRIVING TO my childhood home for my little girl's birthday party. There would be a petting zoo, cake, and ice cream. We were ready to celebrate the life and potential of my little girl, but then the phone rang.

My last grandparent had just past away. She had been rushed to the hospital that morning, and by 5:21 p.m. she died. I didn't know my grandmother that well, but I knew her well enough to wish I had more time with her. She was a caring and gracious woman, the kind this world needs more of. But as I pointed my car toward the party destination, I had a hard time not feeling cheated. How would we celebrate my daughter's three years of life while we begin the slow process of mourning the death of my grandmother?

We live during a time when death is not gone but rather is still intruding as it did before Jesus climbed on the cross. Babies take their first breaths in hospitals where others take their last. Where exactly are we when it comes to this apparent grand solution God has for the suffering and death of this world? How are we supposed to make sense of his promise of death being defeated when all our days seem firmly under death's thumb? If this is indeed a story we are supposed to fit in, where in the story are we? And when will this painful chapter come to a close?

Part IV: Finding Our Story & Place

Our Place in the Story

We live between Genesis 3 and Revelation 21. That is a giant patch of both history past and history future to think about. To say we live between the fall of creation and God's ultimate, unknown future redemption of all things is infuriatingly unhelpful for most of us. We have no illusions about this world still needing to be touched by God's ultimate healing. However, we sometimes need to be reminded.

So much of our anger gets couched in our questioning of why we suffer. Without trying to minimize or moralize the strifes and agonies we experience, some of us forget God is not finished. He tells us there are still many things he wants for this world before putting an end to suffering, shame, and death. Our comments and indignant monologues can sound like someone standing at the end of history instead of our actual place in the process of redemption. If we were screaming about suffering after God had claimed to wipe it all away, our anger would be justified. But we are not there yet: we are here, in the in-between. We are in a place in time where suffering is real and death does more than sting. It bites and rips us apart at times. So again we ask, "Where are we in all of this?"

We are in between groaning and restoration for sure. But something more helpful would be to say that we are between resurrection and resurrection, between Jesus laughing at death's attempt to swallow him and our own joyful outburst standing over death's own grave. We are in a place in the story where promises were made, signs of God's intent to follow through were given, but there has been a long state of waiting. There is a page waiting to be turned, but too many paragraphs still need to be read. We are in a place that continues to wield a hurtful sword. It's a place where faith is still needed. A place where the horizon of hope always seems too far away. It's a place in the story some call "now and not yet."

Now, but Not Yet

It might sound like a cruel joke. Like someone telling you about a great surprise that won't come for a long time. But the idea of "now and not yet" is neither cruel nor a joke. Something happened when Jesus walked out of his grave after three days. It started something, but somehow did not finish it. There was a promise in his vacating that tomb, but promises can take a while to be fulfilled. We live our lives in between this promise given and fully achieved.

If Adam failed in the garden, Jesus didn't. When Jesus prayed in Gethsemane before his death, he was asking for another way, but not at the expense of the Father's will. When the cross was the only way, he stood up to face it. Jesus became the last and true "Adam" because he did what we could not do for ourselves. And when Jesus rose from death to life, he became the first fruits of the eternal race of people we were always intended to be. A redeemed body and soul would now be able to live forever with God because of Jesus. Now there is a present hope Jesus sheds light on. Now is a new time in history. Salvation is now here. The cosmos is now being redeemed and rescued from death and decay. The great enemy and intruder has been defeated . . .

But it is not yet finished. All we have to do is look around and see that things are not all fixed. Death and evil are still very much in this world. The now is not yet complete. As we have seen in different ways already, this "now and not yet" is anything but God's absence or apathy or weakness. Instead, it is his patience and kindness on full display. The fact that we are even believers is the proof. If Jesus died over two thousand years ago, it is because God refused to end this "now and not yet" chapter of history so we could become his children through Jesus's salvation. That is mercy, not absence. Yes, there is also so much pain and sorrow. Yes, people face horrible existences during this time. There is no denying that. And I cannot find answers about this that totally satisfy me, so I will not try to give any to you. Instead, I will only point back to the need for a faith that always seems to grow up beside sorrow and doubt.

Part IV: Finding Our Story & Place

Future Hope, Present Faith

Last chapter we spoke about the beauty of a faith that is big enough to hold both our individual stories and God's own. It's a faith that we do not have to hide ourselves from in order to fit into it. We can be present, even in our doubt and anger. But this is not the end of faith. What if we also came to realize that faith is a burden? He never meant for us to be or feel separated from him. The concept of faith in an unseen or apparently hidden God did not surface in Scripture until after sin and death entered the world. Trust has always been on the table, but groping in the darkness came after death intruded. What does this mean? It means that faith is a burden for all of us who live in this in-between time of "now but not yet."

Faith is a gift. It is not stationary, but it can be halting. It is not misguiding, but it can be so confusing. If we don't come to understand how difficult faith is, we will find ourselves stuck in our demands for answers to our difficult questions. Our suffering will again lead us to think of ourselves as somehow detached from God, or worse, totally abandoned by him. Faith, understood as both a gift and a weight, keeps us hurting believers from destroying ourselves and our relationships with God.

It's hard to remember God's goodness when suffering seems to go unexplained. Instead of feeling some kind of divine whip snap against our backs, we can breathe and wrestle to see the hope that sprung us toward God in the first place. After taking a long look at the old stories that caused pain and bitterness, it's hard to trust that God does truly have a just and sweet plan to resolve what ails. Faith is a gift, but what a burden it is for an imperfect and wounded people as us.

But this burden is not one of despair. We are not Sisyphus rolling a rock of faith up a hill, only to watch it roll back down. Faith has a certain destination. It has an orientation, even for us believers who get lost sometimes. Faith's burden is filled with hope, not despair. We have a hope that God really is who we hear Jesus describe. This hope takes the bite out of the burden. It allows us to somehow find thankfulness that God has hidden some things from us because he wants us to focus more clearly on him. We can even begin to trust him and his "secrets" instead of the suspicion that once turned him into a stranger. We can hope he will see this thing through, even if we hate his timing.

Faith is a burden because we never get all of our questions answered; because pain and decay seem ever-present; because we just don't understand why good people keep dying; because it's inconceivable that rule followers seem to get punished in this world. But faith is a gift because it is a place where hope grows and guides. Yes, faith leads to salvation, but salvation is more than the moment when we somehow move from lost to found, or sinner to saint. Salvation is a progressive movement of our hearts learning to trust God more and more. This progress is long and difficult. Our anger at God has been a part of this process. Our exhaustion, grief, choices, and affections have been caught up in this slow process as well. That is why we have been able to call ourselves both "God-angry" and "believers."

So our place in God's story is located in this in-between time of Jesus paradoxically "now and not yet" bringing about a final healing to all creation. It is a time when both death and new life seem to compete for dominance. This is a place where faith is needed. One day, faith will not be needed because "now and not yet" will just be "now and forever." While knowing where we are in God's story orients us back on our journey, that is only a piece to the whole story. In some ways, we can see it in our surroundings. It is where we live and have been boiling in our anger. Now as we get closer to our journey's end out of our anger, we need to see the *who* and the *how*. *Who* has been inhabiting this place with us, and *how* should we understand our relationship with God? In other words, if we have been short-sighted in our vision of who God is to us, how do we put together all of these different pieces to actually allow us to see this story so we may find it and God beautiful?

Chapter 12

Between Us & Him

WE SEEM TO BE swimming in just as many questions as we were before we started. Now they just sound different. As we come to the end of this walking trail, one question might be the most helpful to answer. It might actually show some of our other questions to be simply masquerading as something other than they are. How do we put all of this information together to understand what God wants us to know about himself, us, and the world? If we can find a way to answer this question, we might have a shot at leaving our anger at God behind. To answer this question, we have to remember a fundamental truth that our anger has helped us forget.

We've Got a Relationship

We've heard it a million times in every church event or group we've been a part of: we have a relationship with God. And the nature of this relationship makes all the difference in the world. How we view God's grace toward us makes us draw conclusions about our relationship with him. If we think he is checking his rule book, then he is that elementary school principal we never liked. If we think he doesn't look our way at all, then he will be mostly absent from the relationship. But if we see him looking at us with pride and acceptance, then we have a relationship with the type of father we always wanted. He is a Father always moving toward us, even when we don't recognize it. But recognizing things anew has been our pattern on this journey.

Many of us have a difficult time with this concept because of our earthly fathers. But what if we could, just for a moment, believe God is a far better father than any that we have met? If we can find a way to suspend our disbelief (even for a moment), I think we might find something astonishing, something we actually want to believe more than our vindictive anger has to offer. The God Jesus reveals to us is a Father who refuses to quit on or let go of his children.

The entire time we have been fighting and yelling at God we have actually been beating on his chest. All this time, we have been thinking God moved far away from us to rot in our sufferings and circumstances, but he has actually been pulling us closer and closer to himself. While we threw our fists toward him, launched verbal assaults, and turned away, he was wrapping us up and speaking softly to us. We couldn't hear him for a variety of reasons (some not our own). And sometimes he did stop speaking to allow us to ramble and yell and tire ourselves out. But we did all of this inside his embrace. Imagine the punishment you would feel if you refused to release a flaying child who saw you as an enemy or stranger holding him down. This is the nature of the relationship we have with God.

Because of Jesus's work, death, and resurrection, we have these royal privileges afforded to us. We can enter the throne room of God without fear or pause. He wants us to run to him and lay out our lives and desires. He wants us to lay it on the line. The good, and oftentimes the ugly. He wants us to risk being rejected for the chance of seeing just how much he accepts us. The curious thing is that God is less interested in us approaching him the "right" way than we are. There is this aspect of God that doesn't let our foolishness get in the way of him seeing the beauty of us being with him. He understands how difficult this life is to navigate. Yes, he wants his glory. Yes, he wants the praise that is due him. Yes, there is a "wrong way" to speak and act toward God, even as a believer. But somehow, God is big enough to see us through our wrongness. And what he sees when he looks at us is Jesus. Because the righteousness that Jesus gives to us, somehow God the Father chooses to find joy in us, even when we are trying to rip ourselves out of his arms.

It is in this relationship where our anger at God unfolds—not in some abstract philosophical or theological crisis about the existence of good and evil. Yes, we have been asking deep questions. But they haven't been asked as part of some passionless research project or a protest rally on a college campus. We have been pleading with God to be who we think he says he is. We are hurt and confused children longing for our Father to help us make sense of things that are either senseless or beyond our abilities to understand. Of course we have come to be suspicious of him. But the faith we could not dismiss kept us hoping that there was something we just didn't know. Something that would help us see that he truly was the good Father he claims to be. This is the relationship with God, child and Father, that will help us put together all that we have seen so far. This is the place, between us and him, where we find how we fit in his grand story.

About These Stories

If God has been holding us in his divine embrace all this time, what about the old stories that we walked through? What about the stories that painfully shaped us? The suffering that became the raw material for our beliefs about the way the universe works? How do we come to bring our lives into some integration inside our relationship with this Heavenly Father?

Our stories are the fodder for the burning questions we have been asking about the suffering and evil we have experienced. Our beliefs found solid foundation in our histories, even if the memories were painful and we tried to forget. As nice as it is that God has been embracing us all this time, we want to know how he can make sense of what seems random, hurtful, and senseless. The short and complicated answer is this: Everything we experience is filtered through the same hands of the Heavenly Father that holds us close to his chest.

There has been nothing we experience that is hidden from God. All of the joy and loss were sifted through his hands into our lives. Yes, he is the author of joy. But, no, he is not the creator of evil. Yes, he sees and allows pain to enter and shape our lives. But, no, he does not enjoy the trauma and decay. Yes, somehow, he is using everything in your life to bring about some eventual and lasting good. But, no, he does not take pleasure in the death and decomposition we have to live through. God has been there through every hardship and whelp this life has doled out. But he has also been there for every good moment in which we dance, every laugh our bellies rolled out. Our lives have been (and will continue to be) a mixed bag of joy and sadness. Mending and tearing. Jumping and crashing. God is always present, always watching, but always looking forward to the greater realities of the larger story we are caught up inside. He is getting his hands dirty in the smallest details while also painting the broad strokes of the total story.

We may never know the answer to all of our *why* questions. We want those answers like our lungs want air. But, the truth is, such knowledge is not as life-giving we want it to be. It is not air. It is not the sustenance that will nourish. Everything will not be all better if we can just understand why terrible things happen to us. Such a truth as this is not satisfying. It might not even be satisfying to hear about how God sometimes allows terrible pain to filter through his hands and into our life. We might still demand that he give us answers for his actions. But he probably won't. Instead, he will probably just continue to hold us and hope for us. He will probably keep allowing joy and dancing to be sprinkled into our days as we live in this in-between time. It might not be satisfying, but we have already crossed this bridge. If faith is a burden of believing things unseen, then there will always be some important and personal questions with missing answers, or unsatisfying ones.

One of the reasons God calls us to walk through our pasts is because he desires us to find the healing and even freedom we have yet to discover. Most of us do everything we can to bury or minimize the past. But both lead to hurt and slavery. Walking through the past is not some magical process. But it does open us up to the places in our stories where we have been scared to grieve, even where we have not trusted God to have any power to heal. All of these moments were used to form beliefs that probably gathered momentum, pushing us to our anger at God. We did not go back through our stories for some morbid exercise. We were looking for places where redemption and joy could begin to grow one day because the land was tilled and not razed.

About His Story

God has been present in this story in which we find ourselves much longer than we have. We know this. We even know that he is the author of the narrative. He is the main character. So how do we make sense and integrate our story into his? How does our place in this history of redemption impact God's story? Because that is what we really want to know. "Do I matter to you, God? Do you care about how much all of this has hurt and wounded me? If so, what are you going to do about it?"

If you were going to write a story about your life, it would probably be pain free. Sure, you would want to be a hero, but without all the risk and struggle. But that is not what God does. This story of his is full of pain and suffering—his own pain and suffering. He has lost more than we have. His wounds go infinitely deeper than ours. He has risked more for the sake of the world than we can imagine. In all of our walks through Jesus's stories, we watched God put himself on the line for the sake of those he loves. We watched God take a stand against evil by letting it kill him. We watched him be mocked and abandoned for the sake of others' rescue. We watched God be a father to thankless and stubborn children who scorn him. Why? Why did the author and main character do this?

He did it for us, and he did it for the entire cosmos. He did it so we could find more in this world than just the pain. He did it so we could find him. God came down into human history to wear skin so we could see him. While there are an infinite number of reasons why God has written this story, there is one that might be most helpful. Once we settle that God's reasons ultimately accomplish his own glory and his people's cosmic redemption, we begin to see that God wrote his story so we could have a way of making sense of our little stories. God did not want us to carry the crushing weight of interpretation on our own. We have been trying to plumb the depths of why sorrow and death exist, but we are running out of air. We have been searching for an explanation to why parents abandon and sickness eats away until we are exhausted. God wants us to see him and his dealing with his creation as a higher and clearer way of interpreting our lives.

We want to know why our history happened to us. We want to know where all of this is going. When will suffering end? Why did this happen to me? In one way or another, God goes about answering our questions with his own story. Why suffering? Because God first suffered the breaking of relationship with one of his rebellious creatures. And that creature wanted to inflict more pain and suffering on God, so he brought sin and death into the world. It might not satisfy because we are still in pain, but think about how God was the first being to ever experience pain, to experience a ruptured relationship. If we look closely enough, we will find more comfort and understanding in the unfathomable story God himself lives. It won't immediately take away the pain. Some of our wounds will need time and care. But it will all happen in the embrace of God. We don't have to hide our pain because he doesn't hide his. We don't have to deny our anger at him. He knows. He doesn't like our anger at him because he knows it's a shallow excuse for the pain we feel. He knows we need grief more than rage, to listen more than talk, talk more than deny, and be still more than run away. His story, like God himself, is holding us in an embrace.

Yes, we have been sinful in our anger at God. Yes, we have been shaking our fists at a version of God that does not accurately portray the God Jesus reveals. Yes, we need to have a holy awe and reverence for God renewed. But this is nothing new. This is a description of all of humanity. We God-angry believers are not

Part IV: Finding Our Story & Place

further gone than any other believer. We are sinful and short-sighted. We have a past that has shaped our beliefs and luggage full of things we need to properly grieve (whatever "properly" means). We need to repent for the choice we made to be angry at God, and we need God to grow our affection for him and his story. We are needy people. And before we begin to walk down an alternative road of justification through self-contempt, we need to remember that we are angry children being held in the embrace of a Heavenly Father that loves us and won't let go . . . even if we never find a way to truly journey out of this anger, we grope toward him.

Bibliography

Allender, Dan B., and Tremper Longman III. *The Cry of the Soul: How Our Emotions Reveal Our Deepest Questions about God.* Colorado Springs: NavPress, 1994. Kindle edition.

Aulen, Gustaf. *Christus Victor: An Historical Study of the Three Main Types of the Idea of Atonement.* Eugene: Wipf & Stock, 2003.

Bird, Michael F. *Evangelical Theology: A Biblical and Systematic Introduction.* Grand Rapids: Zondervan: 2013.

Dr. Seuss. *Oh, the Places You'll Go!* New York: Random House, 1990.

Goldingay, John. *Old Testament Theology: Israel's Faith.* Vol. 2. Downers Grove: InterVarsity, 2006.

Grenz, Stanley J. "Jesus as the Imago Dei: Image-of-God Christology and the Non-Linear Linearity of Theology." *Journal of Evangelical Theological Society* 47 (2004) 617–28.

Jones, Robert D. *Angry at God?* Phillipsburg, NJ: P&R, 2003.

Longman, Tremper, III. *Job.* Baker Commentary on the Old Testament. Grand Rapids: Baker Academic, 2012.

Longman, Tremper, III, and Daniel G. Reid. *God Is a Warrior.* Grand Rapids: Zondervan, 1995.

Macleod, Donald. *The Person of Christ.* Downers Grove: InterVarsity, 1998.

McGrath, Alister E. *What Was God Doing on the Cross?* Eugene: Wipf & Stock, 2002.

Moltmann, Jurgen. *The Crucified God: The Cross of Christ as the Foundation and Criticism of Christian Theology.* Minneapolis: Fortress, 1993.

Piper, Barnabas. *Help My Unbelief: Why Doubt Is Not the Enemy of Faith.* Colorado Springs: Cook, 2015.

Rohr, Richard, and Andreas Ebert. *The Enneagram: A Christian Perspective.* New York: Crossroads, 2001.

Tripp, Paul David. *Instruments in the Redeemer's Hands: People in Need of Change Helping People in Need of Change.* Phillipsburg: P&R, 2002.

BIBLIOGRAPHY

Wright, N. T. *Christians at the Cross: Finding Hope in the Passion, Death, and Resurrection of Jesus*. Ijamsville, MD: Word Among Us, 2007.

———. *Evil and the Justice of God*. Downers Grove: InterVarsity, 2006.

———. *Jesus and the Victory of God: Christian Origins and the Question of God*. London: Society for Promoting Christian Knowledge, 1996.

Yancey, Phillip. *The Question That Never Goes Away*. Grand Rapids: Zondervan, 2014.

www.ingramcontent.com/pod-product-compliance
Lightning Source LLC
Chambersburg PA
CBHW071509150426
43191CB00009B/1461